The Multicolored Mirror:

Cultural Substance in Literature
for Children and Young Adults

The Multicolored Mirror:

Cultural Substance in Literature for Children and Young Adults

Edited by Merri V. Lindgren

Cooperative Children's Book Center

Fort Atkinson, Wisconsin

Published by Highsmith Press
W5527 Highway 106
P.O. Box 800
Fort Atkinson, Wisconsin 53538-0800

The paper used in this publication meets the minimum requirements of American National
Standard for Information Science — Permanence of Paper for Printed Library Material.
ANSI/NISO Z39.48-1984.

ISBN 0-917846-05-2

Library of Congress Card Number: 91-076433

Table of Contents

Preface

Merri V. Lindgren

The Multicolored Mirror: Cultural Substance in Literature for Children and Young Adults, held on April 5-6, 1991, was the eighth children's and young adult literature conference cosponsored by the University of Wisconsin - Madison School of Education, the School of Library & Information Studies and the Cooperative Children's Book Center (CCBC). Soon after it was announced it became obvious that the conference theme was welcomed by participants from the upper Midwest and across the U.S., as the registration maximum was reached long before the scheduled deadline.

Along with inquiries to the CCBC from potential conference-goers came word from representatives of Highsmith Press that they were interested in publishing a book based upon the conference. Duncan Highsmith and Nancy Wilcox of Highsmith Press participated in much of the conference, meeting speakers, and talking with participants. Following the conference our discussion with Highsmith Press continued. An agreement was made to create a book grounded in the conference theme and presentations, but which also expanded upon these ideas. The book would provide a substantial and lasting resource to teachers, librarians, educators, and other interested and involved professionals and adults. In other words, we sought to develop more than just "proceedings," in which the mechanics of a play-by-play transcription often obscure the insight of what was a dynamic dialogue, and leave the reader attempting to conjure up images of what seems—through the reading—like a historical event. Indeed, *The Multicolored Mirror* aims to present strong voices examining a vital concern in a way that stimulates further thought and ongoing discussion.

Content of The Multicolored Mirror

At the Multicolored Mirror conference, as at all CCBC literature conferences, we attempted to offer a range of views on the conference theme from multiple areas of the children's literature community. Virginia Henderson, a psychologist in the Madison Metropolitan School District, discussed the development of self-esteem in children of color. Rudine Sims Bishop talked about evaluating books by and about African-Americans from her perspective as Professor of Education at Ohio State University and author of the ground-breaking book *Shadow and Substance*. Artist

Tom Feelings and photographer George Ancona represented two illustrators' views on cultural authenticity, while authors Elizabeth Fitzgerald Howard, Walter Dean Myers, Gary Soto, and Laurence Yep spoke about writing. Children's librarian, book critic, and poet Doris Seale outlined American history from 1492 to 1992 in a way essential to an understanding of American Indian themes and topics in published materials. Publishers Cheryl and Wade Hudson of Just Us Books and Phoebe Yeh, editor at Scholastic Inc., participated in a panel discussion about publishing. All conference speakers are represented in this book, either through their published work for children or by chapters based on their conference presentations.

In addition to the featured speakers, the conference included small group discussions of children's and young adult books related to the conference theme. Commentaries on the cultural authenticity and accuracy of these 16 books, written by people of the race, culture, or national origin represented in the book being reviewed, are included here. Reflection upon the insights on cultural content within these commentaries can clarify a missing dimension in general children's book reviewing which—too often—contains only enthusiastic descriptions of new books.

Ginny Moore Kruse and Kathleen T. Horning of the Cooperative Children's Book Center expanded their conference presentation of recommended multicultural literature for children and young adults published in 1990 and 1991 to an annotated bibliography of 101 books. They also developed the conference introduction of a brief history of mid-to-late twentieth century multicultural literature for children into a chapter for this book. Appendices include information about an institute for unpublished writers and artists of color held in conjunction with the Multicolored Mirror Conference and a list of professional resources relating to the conference theme.

Definitions and Usage

Throughout the conference and the book we sought for consistent use of terms such as African-American, American Indian, Asian-American, and Hispanic. However, these terms may appear otherwise expressed or punctuated in quotations from outside sources. "Multicultural," a word which suggests various meanings to different people and institutions, has recently come into common usage. At the CCBC and in this book, we define multicultural as referring to people of color, including African-Americans, American Indians, Asian-Americans, and Hispanics. In choosing our terms, we have sought opinions and recommendations of many colleagues and have ultimately tried to select the phrases currently preferred by the people to whom each phrase refers, realizing that this language will continue to evolve over time.

Literary Evaluation Standards

In recommending multicultural books for children and young adults, the CCBC staff follows established high standards for literary and visual excellence, which are applied in all areas of CCBC book evaluation. We look for books which are accurate and interesting, innovative in style, and possess potential appeal to children or young teenagers. We also look for excellent books on themes and topics we know librarians and teachers want and need.

Focus on Multicultural Literature

Delving into a theme that is prevalent in all areas of our society, from literature and film to education and community to politics and economics and beyond, is a challenging and necessary experience. The widespread awareness of this topic was demonstrated in the genesis of the conference theme. Looking back, the conference planning committee found no single impetus leading to the conference theme, but rather several paths: CCBC bibliographic collaboration in the 1960s and 1970s with content specialists such as Fanette Thomas, Daniel Flores Durán, and Janice Beaudin; CCBC staff realization in 1983 that very few books about African-Americans were in print and available for purchase; publisher comments that schools and libraries had already bought all the copies of these books they would ever want; CCBC records showing that in 1985 and 1986 children's publications by African-Americans authors and artists represented less than one percent of all juvenile trade books published, with the numbers for other people of color even lower during this time (with percentages improving only marginally in the intervening years); and, UW-Madison faculty regularly relating the ambiguities which arose in classroom discussions of stereotyping in literature. In addition to all of these factors influencing the decision to plan The Multicolored Mirror, informal conversations in Madison in 1987 with Mavis Jukes, Robert Hudson, Tom Feelings, and Walter Dean Myers had a definite impact upon our thinking, as did the overwhelming national response to the publication of the CCBC's first edition of the bibliography *Multicultural Literature for Children and Young Adults* in 1988. This publication, combined with other factors affecting education and society in general, attracted many requests to the CCBC for information services, as well as for continuing education opportunities about multicultural literature.

In planning the conference and the book, we agreed we wanted to move beyond locating and naming books by and about African-Americans, American Indians, Asian-Americans, and Hispanics. Although the 1991 conference would offer many opportunities to find out about excellent books on the theme, we wanted to do more. We knew that issues of accuracy and authenticity were paramount in any serious consideration of multicultural literature. We decided to address what

Walter Dean Myers calls "cultural substance"—the transmittal of values through culture, and the cultural forces that influence our actions and our lives.

It is unlikely that anyone—regardless of racial, national, cultural, or economic background—will completely agree with everything in this book or anywhere else within the body of writings on multicultural literature. The subject contains the potential for much general misunderstanding. We all lack candor regarding the topic of cultures other than our own. We often do not have the ability to express our real questions and deep concerns. Most of us grow into adulthood with a deep-seated unwillingness to hear another's point of view and follow the hearing with changes in professional behavior, if not also shifts in personal attitude.

Certainly no single conference or book would be expected to resolve the issues, but perhaps the opportunity to hear and read directly from book creators, publishers, and educators of color will deepen a portion of the dialogue underway in the nation during the final decade of the century.

Acknowledgments

We deeply appreciate the support and assistance of the following individuals and groups:

All the conference guest speakers: George Ancona, Rudine Sims Bishop, Tom Feelings, Virginia Henderson, Elizabeth Fitzgerald Howard, Cheryl Hudson, Wade Hudson, Walter Dean Myers, Doris Seale, Gary Soto, Phoebe Yeh and Laurence Yep

Book commentary authors: Cathy Caldwell, Dorothy Davids, Ruth Gudinas, June Kazuko Inuzuka, Yai Lee, Ana Nuncio and Henrietta Smith

Book discussion leaders: Joan Airoldi, Cathy Caldwell, Vernette Crum, Dorothy Davids, Barbara Golden, Ruth Gudinas, Carla Hayden, Josephine Hill, Maureen Holmes, Renée Hoxie, Karen Martin, Henrietta Smith, Holly Willett and Ann Wilson

Conference planning committee: Dianne Hopkins, John M. Kean, Jane Pearlmutter and Holly Willett

CCBC 1990-1991 Advisory Board: Karen M. Algire, Catherine M. Beyers, Vlasta K. Blaha, Jan E. Chambers, Victoria Cothroll, Donald L. Crary, Vernette Crum, Carole DeJardin, LaVonne Ellingson, Miriam Erickson, Mary Louise Gomez, Doris Grajkowski, Josephine D. Hill, Kathleen Hofschield, John M. Kean, Linda Kreft, Ellen Last, Rosemary Leaver, Loretta Life, Susan Mevis, Joan Mish, Rob Reid, Marianne Scheele, Patricia Schutt, John Warren Stewig, and Holly Willett.

CCBC student and volunteer staffs: David Alexander, Elsa Alvarez, Marion Fuller Archer, Inga Banitt, Alice Connors-Suarez, Kim Dahl, Mary Georgeff, Christine Jenkins, Sharon Korbeck, Marie Lundstrom, Megan Schliesman, Sandy Stefaniak, Kristy Sievert and Lynn Silbernagel Sisler

Friends of the CCBC, Inc., especially: Elizabeth Hill Askey, Nancy Beck, Donald L. Crary, Maureen Ellsworth, Sharon Grover, Barbara Huntington, Margaret Jensen, Georgie Palmer, Jane Roeber, Patti Kennelly Sinclair, Laurie Werth, Ann Jarvella Wilson and Laureen Yoshino

Institute for Writers and Artists: Advisory Committee - Cathy Caldwell, Barbara Golden, Karen Martin, Noemi Mendoza, Charles Taylor and Freida High Tesfagiorgis; Consultants - Frances de Usabel, Tom Feelings, Cheryl Hudson, Wade Hudson, Nellie McKay, and Walter Dean Myers

Panel facilitators and speaker introductions: Janice Beaudin, Eliza T. Dresang and Joan Thron

Publisher colleagues: Children's Book Council; HarperCollins, especially William C. Morris; Just Us Books; Houghton Mifflin, especially Peggy Hogan; Henry Holt, especially Christy Smith; Macmillan Children's Book Group, especially Maureen Hayes; Orchard Books, especially Allison Tulloch, and Scholastic/Hardcover

Beverly Slapin of Oyate Books

University of Wisconsin - Extension, especially the Curriculum and Program Development Initiative and Dolores Niles

University of Wisconsin - Madison: Chancellor Donna E. Shalala; School of Education, especially Dean John Palmer, and the Department of Curriculum and Instruction, especially Ann C. Devaney; School of Library and Information Studies/Continuing Education Services, especially Linda Mundt and Marcia Rasmussen; and the University Lectures Committee

University of Wisconsin System, Institute on Race and Ethnicity, especially Director Winston A. Van Horne

Wisconsin Department of Public Instruction: State Superintendent Herbert J. Grover; Division for Library Services, especially Leslyn Shires

Looking into the Mirror:
Considerations behind the Reflections
Kathleen T. Horning and Ginny Moore Kruse

Documenting the Situation

The lack of cultural substance, authenticity, and accuracy in books about people of color has a long, sorry history in the world of U.S. children's literature. Throughout the nineteenth and much of the twentieth century, many published misrepresentations of the histories, cultures, and realities of people of color offered inaccurate and hurtful images. Various editions of "Little Black Sambo" and "The Five Chinese Brothers" represent two familiar examples of stories often recreated inauthentically, even stereotypically.

Beginning in the 1930s, a welcome change was seen with the publication of children's books by African-American authors such as Langston Hughes, Arna Bontemps and Ann Petry. Such books represented the exception rather than the rule in that not-too-distant history of literature published in the U.S. for the young. Dianne Johnson's critical study, *Telling Tales*, analyzes the small body of authentic African-American children's literature published in the early decades of this century. Overall, the lives and works of all people of color continued to be either misrepresented or omitted entirely from the literature published for children in the early and mid-twentieth century.

One cannot underestimate the impact of the leadership of New York Public Library Coordinator of Children's Services Augusta Baker and her NYPL successor Barbara Rollock on behalf of NYPL users and the library community, as well. They conveyed accurate, otherwise unavailable information about excellence in books

Kathleen T. Horning is coordinator of special collections at the CCBC at the University of Wisconsin-Madison and a children's librarian at Madison Public Library. She is the co-author of Multicultural Literature for Children and Young Adults *and editor of* Alternative Press Publishers Of Children's Books: A Directory *(Friends of the CCBC, Inc., 1988 and 1992). She has a B.A. in Linguistics and a Master's Degree in Library and Information Studies, UW-Madison.*

Ginny Moore Kruse is director of the CCBC. She is co-author of Multicultural Literature for Children and Young Adults. *She is a former classroom teacher, school librarian, public librarian and college teacher of children's literature. As part of the CCBC's outreach services, she teaches adult continuing education courses and frequently lectures at the CCBC and elsewhere. She has a B.S. Degree in Education from UW-Oshkosh and a Master's Degree in Library Science from the University of Wisconsin-Madison.*

about African-American themes and topics and about African-American book creators. New York Public Library publications in the mid-twentieth century pointed out the importance of "books for children that give an unbiased, accurate, well-rounded picture of Negro (sic) life in all parts of the world" through various editions of their widely distributed annotated bibliography generally known as *The Black Experience in Children's Books.* The informed introductions to each edition provide unparalleled observations about publishing trends spanning more than four decades.

Chicago Public Library children's librarian Charlemae Rollins developed the publication *We Build Together,* annotated recommendations of books about Black life and literature for elementary and high school use. The first of three editions appeared in 1941 through the auspices of the National Council of Teachers of English.

Publications such as these drew attention to reliable books and, often, to issues concerning the evaluation of children's books about "minorities." Such publications became models for others developed across the nation by major public libraries, professional organizations, school systems, institutions of higher education, and state agencies. For example, Bettye I. Latimer edited *Starting Out Right: Choosing Books about Black People for Young Children* published by the Wisconsin Department of Public Instruction in 1972.

In 1965, educator Nancy Larrick reported on a study she conducted of children's books published by members of the Children's Book Council during the three preceding years. The report appeared in the *Saturday Review,* in an article entitled "The All-White World of Children's Books." She concluded that only four-fifths of one percent of the 5,000 children's books published from 1962-1964 included any mention of contemporary African-Americans in either the words or the pictures. White readers who saw this *Saturday Review* article learned what parents, teachers, and librarians of color had long known: the world of children's books in the early 1960s lacked color. It did not reflect the pluralism of society. The findings in Larrick's academic research corresponded to what Augusta Baker and other practitioners had observed. The study was replicated in a later decade at Harvard University. Larrick's landmark study continues to be cited in late twentieth century reports on the status of multicultural literature for the young, in articles such as "Multicultural Curriculum: African American Children's Literature" by Violet Harris at the University of Illinois.

Larrick's conclusions also had an effect on U.S. children's book publishers and publishing. Dr. Larrick did not find out from anyone inside the publishing community that her study had an impact upon the nature of the books themselves until 25 years after the article appeared in the *Saturday Review.* In 1990, a children's book editor commented informally to Larrick that the increased output during the late 1960s and early 1970s of books showing more sensitivity toward racial diversity could be traced to several factors, one of which most certainly was the *Saturday Review* article by Larrick.

Other factors altered the all-white world of children's books. The initiative of individual children's book editors in actively seeking excellent new writers and artists for all kinds of books can always make a difference in what is ultimately published and in which books become models for new kinds of excellence. For example, Margaret K. McElderry and Jean Karl are among the editors who understood three decades ago that fine artists whose works initially did not encompass commercial book arts could also be book illustrators, without automatically sacrificing artistic standards. Jean Karl visited Ashley Bryan in his studio. Thus began a long association from which Bryan's life-long creation of handmade books for personal gifts and commitment to the traditional arts of his heritage continue to be realized in a distinguished list of distinctive books about African and African-American traditional arts, especially the spirituals and folklore.

In 1967, the Council on Interracial Books for Children (CIBC) was founded in New York City. One of the CIBC's principles held that there were ways to encourage authors and artists of color to create good books for children and to spur publishers to produce and market these books. The CIBC and its dynamic leader Bradford Chambers provided a forum for socially conscious criticism of children's books. Articles and reviews by content specialists, including Rudine Sims (Bishop) and Doris Seale, confronted and challenged the mainstream, mostly white community of teachers, librarians, and publishers with issues concerning cultural substance in media for children and adolescents.

The CIBC also sponsored contests for unpublished writers and illustrators of color. In subsequent years, the list of winners in the CIBC's contests between 1967 and 1979 seems to be almost a "who's who" of contemporary writers of multicultural children's literature: African-American writers Kristin Hunter, Sharon Bell Mathis, Emily Moore, Margaret Musgrove, Walter Dean Myers, and Mildred D. Taylor; American Indian writers Nanabush Chee Dodge and Virginia Driving Hawk Sneve; and Asian-American writers Minfong Ho and Ai-Ling Louie were all winners in the CIBC contests for unpublished writers of color. Each issue of the CIBC's *Bulletin* also included a showcase entitled "Art Directors, Take Note," featuring samples of art by illustrators of color. From this showcase, some publishing house art directors did take note of such artists as Charles Bible, Carole Byard, Donald Crews, Pat Cummings, Leo and Diane Dillon, Cheryl Hanna, and Idalia Rosario. By actively encouraging both children's book creators and children's book publishers throughout the 1970s, the CIBC had a tremendous impact upon the formerly all-white world of children's books. Some of the CIBC's approaches caused considerable discussion and even outrage. Regardless, the

Council on Interracial Books for Children served as a powerful force for change and continues its work in a similar direction.

The Coretta Scott King Award was established in 1969 by Black librarians seeking to formally acknowledge excellence in published writing by Black authors of books for children and young adults. A parallel award was later established for outstanding contributions in illustration by Black artists of books for children. The Coretta Scott King Book Awards are now administered through the Social Responsibilities Round Table of the American Library Association.

Some critics and reviewers contributed significantly throughout the years to the discussion of cultural substance. Rudine Sims (Bishop) conducted a study of books published between 1965 and 1979. The National Council of Teachers of English published her findings in 1982 as a book titled *Shadow and Substance*. In it, she stated:

> At issue is not simply "racial background," but cultural affinity, sensitivity, and sensibility. . . The irony is that as long as people in positions of relative power in the world of children's literature—publishers, librarians, educators—insist that the background of the author does not matter, the opportunities for Black writers will remain limited, since they will have to compete with established non-Black writers whose perspective on the Afro-American experience may be more consistent with that of the editors and publishers and whose opportunities to develop their talents as writers have been greater. [1]

Sims' study offers a convincing argument that familiarity matters, that the background of the author matters, that cultural affinity, sensitivity, and sensibility deeply enrich as well as authenticate the fiction about people of color.

Arlene Hirschfelder's long-term commitment to the evaluation of materials by and about American Indians resulted in widely published articles and books such as the collection of readings *American Indian Stereotypes in the World of Children*. In the late 1980s, Beverly Slapin and Doris Seale's commentaries on books by and about American Indian themes and topics further challenged the community of adults interested in children's literature to look closely at the books about American Indians. Slapin and Seale's publication *Books Without Bias* offered hard-hitting assessments of books containing prevailing notions about American Indians. Slapin and Seale's biting criticism did not spare familiar, favorite children's books such as *The Indian in the Cupboard*, *Knots on a Counting Rope* and *Sign of the Beaver*. Using an approach reminiscent to that of the CIBC, their commentaries angered and confused many readers; the commentaries and articles in *Books Without Bias* also alerted adults looking for books about American Indians to the complexity of evaluation, because Slapin and Seale found very few of the many books about American Indians to recommend.

The CIBC *Bulletin* typically offered exacting appraisals of materials for school-aged children and teenagers about people of color. Usually these appraisals were by content specialists. The CIBC's emphasis upon extraliterary evaluation seemed to leave little, if any, room for standard evaluation criteria involving literary and artistic excellence. CIBC *Bulletin* media evaluations were particularly harsh concerning the authenticity of published voices originating outside of direct experience. CIBC articles and reviews continued to offer examples of what Sims found in her study: the greater the distance between direct familiarity and experience with the subject, the greater the creative challenge for the writer, artist, publisher, and reviewer working with material from outside his/her personal background or cultural experience. Although these concerns are not always welcome within the children's book community, the Council on Interracial Books for Children provided and continues to provide a consistent forum where such concerns are represented.

Publishing of multicultural literature for children and young adults expanded throughout the late 1960s and early 1970s, reflecting a growing recognition of the diversity of an increasingly pluralistic society, as well as the social consciousness of the U.S. Civil Rights Movement. Gifted authors and illustrators of color created books out of their own experiences. Of the manuscripts that were published, voices previously unheard in youth literature became available to all children. The new combination of book consumer and book publisher demand for authentic literature for all children reflecting the lives of children of color opened the door to many fine authors and illustrators whose first works for children were published during this time. In addition to the book creators already cited, they included Lucille Clifton, Alice Childress, Muriel Feelings, Tom Feelings, Eloise Greenfield, Rosa Guy, Julius Lester, Nicholasa Mohr, Jerry Pinkney, John Steptoe, and Laurence Yep. A brief review of some of the books published reveals the wide range and depth of publishing during that time.

Yoshiko Uchida wrote of growing up in the United States as a Japanese-American child during World War II in *Journey to Topaz* and *Journey Home*. Laurence Yep provided a Chinese-American point of view in many of his books, including *Dragonwings*, *Child of the Owl*, and *Sea Glass*. Ed Young illustrated Jane Yolen's original story, *The Emperor and the Kite*, and continued to express many dimensions of Chinese culture in his books published during succeeding decades. He was the U.S. nominee for the 1992 International Board on Books for Young People Hans Christian Andersen Award for the body of his children's book illustration.

Nicholasa Mohr wrote about Puerto Rican-American life in her short fiction for younger adolescents, *El Bronx Remembered* and *In Nueva York*, and in her novels for young readers. In Cruz Martel's picture book, *Yagua Days*, the rare portrait of a Puerto Rican-American family was seen through the experience of a young boy's delight in a reunion with his relatives in Puerto Rico.

American Indian authors were and are seldom represented in the world of mainstream corporate publishing for youth. Virginia Driving Hawk Sneve's novels such as *Betrayed* and *Jimmy Yellow Hawk* offer reliable historical and cultural perspectives.

Many of the African-American authors and illustrators who were first published in the late 1960s and early 1970s continue to account for the majority of culturally authentic books about African-American experience which enrich U.S. children's literature during the late twentieth century. The award-winning author Virginia Hamilton writes substantial nonfiction, as in her biographical works *Paul Robeson* and *Anthony Burns*. She created complex novels for older children such as *Arilla Sun Down* in which she experimented with narrative style. Hamilton's third novel *The Planet of Junior Brown* was a Newbery Honor Book. *M. C. Higgins, the Great* won the Newbery Medal, the Boston Globe/Horn Book Award and the National Book Award, making Hamilton the only author ever to win three major children's book awards for distinguished writing for a single title. Virginia Hamilton became the U.S. nominee for the 1992 International Board on Books for Young People's Hans Christian Andersen Award for the entirety of her written works.

CIBC contest winner Sharon Bell Mathis showed great skill in depicting the unstated tension in contemporary families in *Teacup Full of Roses*, *Listen for the Fig Tree* and in her hauntingly beautiful Newbery Honor Book, *The Hundred Penny Box*.

Mildred D. Taylor was also the winner of a CIBC contest. Beginning with *Song of the Trees* and continuing through Newbery Medal winner *Roll of Thunder, Hear My Cry*, Taylor created and began to follow her protagonist Cassie Logan through childhood and through social changes in the rural South during the segregation of the 1930s and early 1940s.

Poet Lucille Clifton wrote the texts for over a dozen picture books in the 1970s, in addition to two short novels, *The Times They Used to Be* and *The Lucky Stone*. A marvelous sequence playfully and poetically illuminates universal childhood experience through the eyes of Everett Anderson, a child who appears in *Everett Anderson's Nine Month Long*, *Everett Anderson's Year*, and other books created by Clifton. Clifton's *All of Us Come Cross the Water* illustrated by John Steptoe featured a young boy turning to an adult mentor in his community to find out about the history of African-American people when he couldn't get the answers he wanted in his school classroom.

Eloise Greenfield writes in a variety of genres, including picture book texts such as *She Come Bringing Me that Little Baby Girl* and *Africa Dream*; novels (*Sister* and *Talk about a Family*); poetry (*Honey, I Love* and *Nathaniel Talking*); biographies (*Rosa Parks* and *Paul Robeson*); and autobiography (*Childtimes*) co-authored with her mother Lessie Jones Little.

Walter Dean Myers, CIBC contest winner in 1968, generally writes wry and witty novels picturing contemporary urban life; they include *Fast Sam, Cool Clyde, and Stuff* and *The Young Landlords*. Myers' published works for children and young adults, his speeches and articles about the representation of the African-American experience in juvenile trade publishing, and his concern for new writers mark him as both an imagemaker (Sims) and a change agent in these times.

Complexities Concerning Evaluation of Cultural Substance

A single formula or checklist will not successfully encompass the intangibles present within the literary arts. Facile answers cannot be found regarding the evaluation of literature created for the young which is, in one way or another, about people whose lives are bi-cultural in terms of their history, culture, or experience. This is a hard reality for publishers, reviewers, librarians, teachers, parents, and others looking for excellent books with authentic cultural elements.

Until very recently, inauthentic images and content concerning people of color were generally not noted as a matter of course by people outside of their own specific race or culture. Most children's book editorial departments were composed of people whose backgrounds were Euro-American. Most children's and young adult book review journals utilized reviewers whose understandings of races and cultures other than their own were shaped by the prevailing images and ideas in the dominant culture. Most teachers and librarians likewise brought a lack of cultural experience to their professional work. It is now clear that a devastating lack of information and insight about cultures (other than their own and the dominant culture) was provided to professionals through formal education or through incidental exposure to the images within society. For these and for countless other reasons as well, the overall nature of books reaching children through the mechanisms of the U.S. children's book community was, until very recently, still almost as "all-white" as it was reported to be in Larrick's study.

Renewed Attention to Multicultural Children's and Young Adult Literature

Although awareness grew throughout the last half of the twentieth century, during the late 1980s an increasing number of teachers, librarians, and parents from varied racial and cultural backgrounds recognized that no child is equipped for the present or for the future without opportunities to see a multicolored society reflected in books and other media. From the evidence of their active searching in libraries and book stores for such materials, it became increasingly clear within the children's book world that contemporary media had frequently misrepresented or omitted the histories, cultures, and contemporary lives of most people of color. The knowledge that institutionalized racism is a complex, world-wide issue involving all ages and stages of life and affecting more than the creation of materials for children and young teenagers did not daunt the people concerned to locate the best for the youth for whom they had responsibility. People committed to cultural diversity exerted greater effort to locate reliable multicultural literature. People working directly with today's youth recognized the importance of providing all children and teenagers with culturally authentic materials. Librarians and teachers stepped up their search for accurate information and authentic materials by and about people of color. Many libraries and school districts supported these efforts with funds for materials and staff time for continuing education about multicultural literature. National professional organizations planned and held programs on the subject, and additional professional material identifying books deemed to be "multicultural" in some respect was published. The children's book community began to realize that a fair evaluation of books by and about people of color involves more than what had been previously attempted. The lack of unanimity and the absence of facile formulas could not excuse disengagement from the dialogue.

A new and renewed commitment to creating and publishing multicultual literature became apparent during the early 1990s. The talent for creating these books was there, as it always has been. Adults from a variety of backgrounds became actively involved in creating books with cultural substance for children and young teenagers.

New ways of publishing developed. CCBC collection development and CCBC work with alternative press publisher information since 1980 offers a vantage point for recognition of the rapidly increasing number of small independent publishers of color developing children's books as part or all of their output. A fast-growing network established by the Multicultural Publishers Exchange (MPE) issues a regular newsletter and furnishes a variety of business and educational services to MPE members. The first national MPE conference was held in 1990 in Madison, Wisconsin.

New configurations of large publishers continued to be forged during the early 1990s. The broadening range of book packager services to large publishers generated new possibilities for reaching targeted markets with books. Many corporately owned book publishers expanded the number of new "multicultural" titles published each season during 1991. Some of these publishers also actively promoted backlists advertised as multicultural.

Some of the trade publishers and national professional groups planned ways to encourage writers and artists of color to submit unpublished manuscripts and art.

Writers and artists of the 1990s continued to wrestle with the complex challenges of creating images, stories, narratives, and accounts which range in content and theme, within as well as beyond their direct experiences. As Sims' study points out, Euro-American book creators often gain the commercial opportunity to create books about people of color. The published works of writers and artists of color indicated that, in the past, they may have been limited by forces within or beyond themselves to topics close to their direct experience. Like their white counterparts, they also wish to use their gifts to serve the story or the exposition of themes and topics beyond their direct experience; they typically have a working knowledge of the dominant culture from the standard curriculum, if not from direct experience.

Once published, books must be promoted through standard means as well as through untapped networks of potential consumers. The old assumption that multicultural literature will not fare well in retail book stores must be re-examined over time by publishers and booksellers committed to actively promoting this literature year-round. The quality and quantity of the multicultural content of the new books as well as the publisher backlists and promotional materials at the beginning of the twenty-first century will demonstrate the extent and depth of the current publishing commitment to multicultual literature.

High standards must be applied to the evaluation of all books, as always. Evaluation criteria must always make room for any book to be valued for what it is, for the way in which it is unique, and for what it contributes, as well as commenting upon whether or not this was accomplished. Professional reviews of any books concerning racial issues must increase in reliability and specificity to guide librarians, teachers, and parents.

Continuing the Active Search and Use of Multicultural Literature

Insight and experience about races and cultures other than one's own can be found by anyone who wants to make the effort. Adults who create, select, and share books for direct use with children are encouraged to expand their commitment to the search for excellent multicultural literature, rather than to merely accumulate ever-growing lists of books identified by one means or another as "multicultural." Midst everything else vying for their time and energy, these adults are invited and urged to make a regular commitment to reading and knowing works beyond their personal backgrounds for general use with all children during all months of the year, rather than only during special observances. The more voices to which one truly listens through such reading, the more one begins to be able to distinguish authenticity of cultural substance from that which is superficially "multicultural."

Society in general does not adequately prepare youth and adults to engage in a formal, constructive way with matters concerning race. Readers are urged to be open to ideas other than those with which they feel initially comfortable. They will be called to act upon reliable, new insights about books which have long been personal or professional favorites; finding out that such books may be good stories but do not measure up in accurate representation of a culture or race requires change. Change is difficult and inconvenient, but change on behalf of all youth is possible and necessary. It is also exciting! Only as adults continue to discover truly excellent multicultural books first-hand and discover among these books the ones about which they are genuinely enthusiastic will some of the superior multicultural literature published in the past, in these times, and in the future become the books which are actively and regularly called to the listening and reading attention of all children and young teenagers.

June Jordan referred to cultural substance when she wrote of the "multicolored mirror of an honest humankind" in her moving work *Who Look at Me*.[2] Who, indeed, does look? Who and what can be seen? What images will children see when they open the books in their classrooms, libraries and homes? Will they see themselves? Will they see an unrealistic all-white or predominantly white world? Will they see untrue images of their own culture? Or will they see, as Arnold Adoff expresses in his poem, "all the colors of the race — human, of course."[3]

Notes:

1. Sims, *Shadow and Substance*, 13-14.

2. Jordan, *Who Look at Me*, 24.

3. Adoff, "All the colors of the race," in *All the Colors of the Race*, 5.

Works Cited:

Adoff, Arnold. "All the colors of the race." *All the Colors of the Race*. Illustrated by John Steptoe. New York: Lothrop, Lee & Shepard, 1982.

Banks, Lynn Reid. *The Indian in the Cupboard*. Illustrated by Brock Cole. New York: Doubleday, 1980.

Clifton, Lucille. *All of Us Come Cross the Water*. Illustrated by John Steptoe. New York: Holt, Rinehart and Winston, 1973.

———. *Everett Anderson's Nine Month Long*. Illustrated by Ann Grifalconi. New York: Holt, Rinehart and Winston, 1978.

———.*Everett Anderson's Year*. Illustrated by Ann Grifalconi. New York: Holt, Rinehart and Winston, 1974.

———. *The Lucky Stone*. Illustrated by Dale Payson. New York: Delacorte, 1979.

———.*The Times They Used to Be*. Illustrated by Susan Jeschke. New York: Holt, Rinehart and Winston, 1974.

Greenfield, Eloise. *Africa Dream*. Illustrated by Carole Byard. New York: John Day, 1977.

———, and Lessie Jones Little. *Childtimes*. Illustrated by Jerry Pinkney. New York: Crowell, 1979.

———. *Honey, I Love*. Illustrated by Diane and Leo Dillon. New York: Crowell, 1972.

———.*Nathaniel Talking*. Illustrated by Jan Spivey Gilchrist. New York: Black Butterfly, 1988.

———. *Paul Robeson*. Illustrated by George Ford. New York: Crowell, 1974.

———. *Rosa Parks*. Illustrated by Eric Marlow. New York: Crowell, 1973.

———. *She Come Bringing Me that Little Baby Girl*. Illustrated by John Steptoe. Philadelphia: Lippincott, 1974.

———. *Sister*. Illustrated by Moneta Barnett. New York: Crowell, 1974.

———. *Talk about a Family*. Illustrated by James Calvin. Philadelphia: Lippincott, 1978.

Hamilton, Virginia. *Anthony Burns: The Defeat and Triumph of a Fugitive Slave*. New York: Knopf, 1988.

———. *Arilla Sun Down*. New York: Greenwillow, 1976.

———. *M. C. Higgins, the Great*. New York: Macmillan, 1974.

———. *Paul Robeson: The Life and Times of a Free Man*. New York: Harper & Row, 1974.

———. *The Planet of Junior Brown*. New York: Macmillan, 1971.

Harris, Violet. "Multicultural Curriculum: African American's Children's Literature." *Young Children* 46, no. 2 (January 1991): 37-44.

Hirschfelder, Arlene B. *American Indian Stereotypes in the World of Children: A Reader and Bibliography*. Metuchen, NJ: Scarecrow Press, 1982.

Johnson, Dianne. *Telling Tales: The Pedagogy and Promise of African American Literature for Youth*. Westport, Conn.: Greenwood, 1990.

Jordan, June. *Who Look at Me*. New York: Crowell, 1969.

Kruse, Ginny Moore, and Kathleen T. Horning. *Multicultural Literature for Children and Young Adults: A Selected Listing of Books 1980-1990 by and about People of Color*. 3d ed. Madison, Wis.: Wisconsin Department of Public Instruction, 1991.

Larrick, Nancy. "The All-White World of Children's Books." *Saturday Review* (September 11, 1965): 63-65, 84-85.

Latimer, Bettye I., editor. *Starting Out Right: Choosing Books about Black People for Young Children: Preschool through Third Grade*. Bulletin N. 2314. Wisconsin Department of Public Instruction, 1972.

Martel, Cruz. *Yagua Days*. Illustrated by Jerry Pinkney. New York: Dial, 1976.

Martin, Bill, Jr. *Knots on a Counting Rope*. Illustrated by Ted Rand. New York: Henry Holt, 1987, 1966.

Mathis, Sharon Bell. *The Hundred Penny Box*. Illustrated by Leo and Diane Dillon. New York: Viking, 1975.

———. *Listen for the Fig Tree*. New York: Viking, 1974.

———. *Teacup Full of Roses*. New York: Viking, 1972.

Mohr, Nicholasa. *El Bronx Remembered*. New York: Harper & Row, 1975; Houston, Tex.: Arte Publico, 1986.

———. *In Nueva York*. New York: Dial, 1977; Houston, Tex.: Arte Publico, 1988.

Myers, Walter Dean. *Fast Sam, Cool Clyde, and Stuff*. New York: Viking, 1975.

———. *The Young Landlords*. New York: Viking, 1979.

New York Public Library. *The Black Experience in Children's Literature*. New York Public Library, 1989. Former titles: *Books about Negro Life for Children* (1957 and 1963); *The Black Experience in Children's Books* (1971, 1974 and 1984).

Rollins, Charlamae. *We Build Together: A Reader's Guide to Negro Life and Literature for Elementary and High School Use*. Champaign, IL: National Council of Teachers of English, 1967.

Sims, Rudine. *Shadow and Substance: Afro-American Experience in Contemporary Children's Fiction*. Urbana, Ill.: National Council of Teachers of English, 1982.

Slapin, Beverly, and Doris Seale. *Books without Bias: Through Indian Eyes*. Berkeley, Cal.: Oyate, 1988.

Sneve, Virginia Driving Hawk. *Betrayed*. New York: Holiday House, 1974.

———. *Jimmy Yellow Hawk*. Illustrated by Oren Lyons. New York: Holiday House, 1972.

Speare, Elizabeth George. *Sign of the Beaver*. Boston: Houghton Mifflin, 1983.

Taylor, Mildred D. *Roll of Thunder, Hear My Cry*. New York: Dial, 1976.

———. *Song of the Trees*. Illustrated by Jerry Pinkney. New York: Dial, 1975.

Uchida, Yoshiko. *Journey Home*. Illustrated by Charles Robinson. New York: Atheneum, 1978.

———. *Journey to Topaz: A Story of the Japanese-American Evacuation*. Illustrated by Donald Carrick. New York: Scribner, 1971.

Yep, Laurence. *Child of the Owl*. New York: Harper & Row, 1977.

———. *Dragonwings*. New York: Harper & Row, 1975.

———. *Sea Glass*. New York: Harper & Row, 1979.

Yolen, Jane. *The Emperor and the Kite*. Illustrated by Ed Young. Cleveland: World Publishing, 1967.

The Development of Self-esteem in Children of Color

Virginia M. Henderson, Ph.D.

We all come to any experience carrying perceptions of our own personal reality, developed through the experiences of living. That personal reality may be somewhat different than the reality with which we are actually confronted. Our perceptions of who we are have grown out of our understanding of how we are perceived and treated by others. Other people may see the same reality that we do, but perceive it differently. Unless we are challenged to change perceptions to fit reality, it is far more comfortable and simpler to accept our own perceptions as unshakable fact. Those challenges are crucial in our understanding of our perceptions of ourselves and of others, and in the development of self-esteem. I would like to consider the self-esteem of children, particularly children of color, from different points of view. Self-esteem is about perceptions and it is also about freedom. It is about freedom for us to be who we are. Langston Hughes, in his poem, "Freedom," writes:

> *Freedom will not come*
> *Today, this year*
>   *Nor ever*
> *Through compromise and fear.*
>
> *I have as much right*
> *As the other fellow has*
>   *To stand*
> *On my own two feet*
> *And own the land.*

Virginia Henderson is a psychologist and the chair of the Minority Student Achievement Committees and Initiatives in the Madison Metropolitan School District. She earned degrees from Spelman College, Boston University, and the University of New Mexico. She was a member of the faculty in the Department of Pediatrics and Psychiatry at the University of New Mexico - School of Medicine. She lives in Madison, Wisconsin.

I tire so of hearing people say,
Let things take their course.
Tomorrow is another day.
I do not need my freedom when I'm dead.
I cannot live on tomorrow's bread.

Freedom
Is a strong seed
Planted
In a great need.
I live here, too.
I want freedom
Just as you.[1]

"Freedom" could very well be the title of this chapter—freedom for children of color to grow up in a world that values them and their racial, cultural, and ethnic heritage and authentically represents them in all aspects of life. Who are the children of color? For my purpose here, they will be defined as African-American, Hispanic/Latino, Asian and Pacific Islander, American Indian, and Alaskan Native. A note of caution: there are many differences within and among these groups including religions, languages, dialects, and cultural foci. Not to recognize this is to continue the damaging stereotypes of the past.

A 1988 NEA Report, ". . . And Justice For All," written by people of color about themselves, their needs, their hopes, and their dreams, was the basis for the following descriptions of children of color. I will weave my scenario about the mythical child, born today, with the descriptions of the groups provided in the NEA Report.

An African-American child born today will greet a world where racism, sexism, classism, handicapism, and a variety of other "-isms" continue to be subtly and blatantly at work. This child will join over 10 million other African-American children in the U.S. This child will be born 126 years after the Emancipation Proclamation officially freed the slaves, but only 37 years since the historic *Brown versus Board of Education of Topeka* where the U.S. Supreme Court ruled that segregated schools were inherently inferior. A child born today will find 50 percent of African-American children living where there is a high concentration of poverty, and they may experience all or most of the devastating effects that poverty brings. This child may have a mother who has had little or no prenatal care, but might also have a mother who is one of the growing numbers of those who has had adequate health care. There is a high probability that the mother may be a teenager. This child will be born into a world where incidents involving drugs, disease, and crime are higher for their own racial group than for other groups of color. There is a high probability that this child will be born into a home headed by a female. While this is not unusual for the African-American family, extended family ties are weakening. Despite these factors, the African-American family is surviving, but the strength of this survival has not been legitimately nor adequately emphasized in the telling of our history.

This child will be born into a world where, despite all of the above characteristics and trends, families continue to see education as crucial even though it may or may not have fulfilled the dreams of the parents. This child will be born into a world with a growing African-American middle class, and into a world in which there are children who are young and gifted but often not challenged as they should be. It is a world still struggling with issues of equity and equality.

The good news? If this child survives the educational system and is not retained or put in special education, he or she will graduate in the class of the year 2009 in the twenty-first century. What will that world look like for this child? How will this child be able to compete? Is the development of self-esteem in children of color different from that of other children?

An Hispanic-American child born today will be born into the fastest growing ethnic group in this country. He or she may be a child whose family is native to the United States or they may be immigrants. Whichever they are, their contributions to the growth of America have been important and substantial. Although Hispanic people have a common Spanish culture, religion, and language, "there are significant differences among the Hispanics due to their reasons for emigration or their national origins."[2] This infant will be born into a world where the drop-out rate for Hispanic youth is high, a world where Hispanic male students work more hours per week while attending school than students of any other group. As with other groups of color, Hispanic children will be under-represented in higher education. Still, as with the other groups, Hispanic parents understand the need for and want a good education for their children. Although discrimination and cultural differences are often identified as barriers to success, the greater obstacles are poverty and limited English proficiency, and as with the other racial/ethnic groups of color, the devastating effects of poverty on their lives are significant. If successful, this Hispanic child will also graduate from high school in the year 2009. Given these circumstances for the Hispanic child, what might be the status of his or her self-esteem?

An American Indian or Alaskan Native infant born today will find a world in which parents have many concerns about the future of their child. This child will find a world in which their authentic history has yet to be told in a consistent manner. He or she will be born into a world in which the historical understanding of their treaty rights is still in controversy. Again, there would be no question that education is important to the parents and to the tribal leaders. "As the original inhabitants of the United States, Indians also claim rights accruing to no other group of Americans."[3] This has resulted in ongoing tensions. It is critical that we learn the importance and implications of these treaties. It is imperative that the American Indian culture and the family unit be preserved. "Enhancing of self concept of Indian students is essential to the effective education of Indian students. Helping students recognize their heritage, giving them a sense of belonging, as well as a sense of their uniqueness as Indians, is essential."[4] What level of self-esteem can an American Indian child develop when there are conflicts that affect their very livelihood and the preservation of their traditions is constantly under attack or challenged? However, if successful, this child will also be a member of a high school graduating class in the year 2009.

An Asian or Pacific Islander child born today may be born into one of many different ethnic groups, and of many different languages. The NEA report previously cited states that Asian and Pacific Islanders come from a multitude of cultures and political, religious, and economic backgrounds, as do other people of color. "The differences among Asian and Pacific Islander groups are exacerbated by the length of time each group has been exposed to Western ways. This child's family may meet prejudice for similar as well as for different reasons as those children born into other groups of color . . . . Asian and Pacific Islander families who are American-born and long term residents of the United States have problems that closely resemble the problems of white youth in our country. Immigrants and refugee youth may have problems with language, cultural adjustment, economic survival, and the psychological scars of war."[5] Regardless of which family this child is born into, a good education is top priority. Many of their parents came to this country for educational opportunities which are stressed in the family. This attitude has put considerable pressure on children who do not feel that they can live up to these expectations of high academic achievement. This particular group often suffers from the stereotypic myths of the high achieving model minority, affecting the self-esteem of those who cannot meet these standards, while those who do are often criticized by people outside of their families. If these children born today survive and are successful, they too will complete high school in the year 2009. What will it be like for them?

These are our children of color. A diverse group, indeed. The complexities and richness of their diverse cultural heritages also have many human and situational commonalities which will affect their developing concept of self.

The children of color are children first and foremost. Their course in life may be different than yours, but they have the same basic needs as do all children. I hope the previous discussion of what a child of color born today will face gives us a view to think about. I believe it will help us to understand the enormous diversity within and among groups, and the challenges that they face because they are identifiably "different." If these children of color are successful and graduate from high school in 2009, they are going to find a dramatically different world in which they and their families will collectively comprise over one-third of this nation. Will that make a significant difference in the way they are perceived by themselves and by others? However, when we look at our history, 18 years is a small amount of time, so we don't have time to waste. We have to get busy making this a world in which we are all valued.

I began by discussing self-esteem. Now let us look at some of its definitions. I quickly became frustrated as I looked through the literature and realized that there are many, many definitions of self-esteem. Words such as self-worth, self-esteem, and self-identity were used in an interrelated manner. All of these words can apply here. Virginia Satir, the late noted family therapist, once said, "Feelings of worth can flourish only in an atmosphere where individual differences are appreciated, where mistakes are tolerated, where communication is open, and the rules are flexible; the kind of atmosphere that is found in a nurturing family."[6] Indeed, self-esteem and self-worth are born and nurtured in the family. The family is described as the child's first teacher, and schools as the child's formal teacher. Using a developmental context for understanding, we can see how both family and school are critical in the development of self-esteem. Researchers vary on whether or not this is something we can measure and how it can be measured. Arlene Kagle, a psychologist in New York, says about self-esteem, "It can't be measured on a scale because it is different things to different people. High self-esteem is simply being comfortable in your own skin and feeling you are a valuable person. A strong foundation gives an individual the resilience to bounce back from life's large and small failures, and the ability to make choices confidently . . . . Self-esteem develops from a complex interaction of messages passed on by parents and society."[7]

Three personal stories illustrate the importance of family. I am an identical twin. My father was a minister. When my two older brothers wanted a sister, he told them to pray. Each of their prayers was answered. (They tell us that it was their last prayer.) My parents were educated, but in those days in Cleveland, Ohio, we had to constantly verify the fact that they were, because people didn't understand that African-Americans could have college educations. We were good students but we were often surprised at some teachers' amazement over how well we could achieve.

My father said to us repeatedly as we became adolescents, "Daughters, you are going to have to do twice as much to go half as far." When we questioned him, he said, "You're going to have to do this because you are Negro and because you are women." We argued these points with him but he continued by saying, "It is not going to be easy, but with the help of your family and our God, you can be anything you want to be." That was a very strong message. Although we sometimes rebelled against it because being different was hard, we remembered. I have never forgotten what he said, and I think it was important for many reasons. First, our parents foreshadowed problems for us and offered solutions and support. As a family, we talked about race, we talked about being different, and we talked about high expectations. Among all that conversation, we learned that it was important to be who we were. It is a tragedy that there are so many parents out there who want the same thing for their children but are unable to provide the kind of opportunities and models for success that they would like for their children. Many parents want their children to have high self-esteem and opportunities but are unable for many reasons to give them the kind of message to support it. Often, that message wasn't given to the parents themselves. Consider their self-esteem.

What are some of the challenges for providing opportunities and models for learning the positive messages about ourselves? Multicultural literature, the kind which tells of the struggles, myths, movement, beauty, rituals, religion, and holidays of our people, is important. We all need to know these things. Remember, it is from others that we begin to form our perceptions of ourselves. The building of self-esteem is a developmental process and during the process, our self-esteem undergoes change. We change our opinions of who we are over and over again as we develop into the person we are to become.

Margaret Spencer, in the book entitled *Beginnings*, makes several very important points about the social and affective development of Black children. Ms. Spencer believes that self-esteem can be measured, and that it must be examined from a developmental perspective. She reports children of color have historically been studied in a static manner as mere reactors to twentieth century racism. She believes that, "the life span, or the developmental view, is a more inclusive perspective for examining identity issues. The approach emphasizes the biological, historical, sociocultural, and psychological factors that provide a context for explaining behavior from birth to death. There have been few attempts to interface the cognitive with the affective domain. Dependent on the child's developmental stage, experiences, and underlying cognitive structures, different categories of self should emerge and disappear over time. Without personal/psychological or extrinsic/sociocultural intervention, the expected course of the Black child's identity is toward an identity imbalance—an identity imbalance characterized by a non-fit between personal and group identity."[8] The discordance between the child of color and the world in which they live within their families, as contrasted to the world in which they must live as they move beyond their communities, forms a misfit that many of us do not consider when we talk about the behaviors, the attitudes, and abilities of children of color.

Ms. Spencer goes on to say that she believes that "society's perception of minorities has remained essentially unchanged, although those perceptions may vary in form."[9] What does this say for our developing child of color, what hope is there for change, and what does it say for our graduates of the year 2009? In other words, racism cuts at the very heart and very sense of self in the developing child of color. We know that it presents barriers to the attainment of many goals, as has been demonstrated over and over again through the years.

Sparks, Gutierrez, and Phillips in their article, "Teaching Young Children to Resist Bias — What Parents Can Do," explain that "the two major tasks of early childhood are developing self-identity and self-esteem, and developing skills for social interaction . . . . What children learn in the preschool years greatly influences whether they will grow up to value themselves, accept and comfortably interact with diverse people, or whether they will succumb to the biases that result in or help to justify unfair treatment of an individual because of their identity."[10]

Many of us are amazed to learn that prejudices, biases, and differences are already formed by the age of three, and certainly by the age of four. At this young age, they are able to recognize differences and to know which are positive and negative, although it is not yet within their framework of prejudice due to their immature cognitive level. Just go to a nursery school or preschool and watch and listen to the children playing in the doll corner. You will be surprised to hear all kinds of clearly articulated opinions, stereotypes, and prejudices and to watch them dramatically and behaviorally displayed.

Two other personal experiences illustrate this developmental process. At the time my family experienced these episodes, my daughters were three and three and one-half, respectively. Our oldest daughter was bussed to her nursery school every day. Unknown to us, the children were making fun of her by calling her "Mud Face." She never told us about this, and we only learned when a white parent called and said that she had seen to it that the bus driver was fired because he had tolerated such behavior on his bus. Of course, I was horrified and angry. My husband and I sat down with our daughter and asked her about the name-calling. She looked at us in amazement. She did not see it as a bad thing, indeed, she was enjoying the attention being drawn to her egocentric self. She knew she was "brown" because we had talked about how different our color was from that of her playmates. She also loved to play in mud, so what was the problem? As a parent, I knew that I had a job to do. My daughter's perception was different from my own, and rightfully so. As I have thought about it over time, I think that perhaps it was developmentally appropriate for a three year old to feel positive about an act that made her the center of attention, which for us, as adults, seemed vicious.

A couple of years later, we had another episode. Our younger daughter was always sensitive to rejection from whatever source it came. We lived in a community where she looked out onto an essentially white world. Many of her friends were white and had blonde hair. One day at the age of three, she came storming and screaming into the house, announcing that she wanted blonde hair. Not only blonde hair, she wanted to be white *right now*. As a parent, what could I do about that? She said that everybody she knew had blonde hair, and she yelled, "I'm ugly." What self rejection she was expressing because of her difference. As I thought about it, I realized that in her preschool environment the dolls were white, there were no pictures of children of color on the walls, and no illustrations of children of color in the books. In her own effort to make my child feel accepted at school as one of two Black children, the teacher called her, "My precious little Hershey Bar."

As a parent, I had a job to do. I did not question my children's perceptions, but I did work with their reality. In fact, they were Black, they were different, we were a different kind of family, but it was all right. My youngest daughter's self-esteem, however, was very low, and her very being was challenged when she said, "I am ugly." As parents, my husband and I had done everything we thought we could do. In many ways, we tried to expose our children to their roots and their cultures. We attended a Black church. We had images of many persons of color in our home, as well as friends of color. We read poems by Black authors and wrote our own plays about our people. But for this daughter, it was not enough. As I thought about it further, perhaps she was saying, "I do not see myself reflected anywhere but at home, and that is not good enough, because I exist in places outside of home. Does this mean that I do not exist as an acceptable person except to my family?" That was her perception of herself at that time. Let us understand that to be a family of color, under stress, often with few resources or skills, does not mean that we do not care about, do not love, do not nurture our children. We care very, very deeply.

Since we believe that the developmental approach is a valid way to look at development of self, let's take a brief walk through this process. The development of self-esteem begins at birth. If well nurtured, infants begin to sense that someone cares for them and that their basic needs are being fulfilled, they begin to build a sense of trust that the world is good, and as a result, that they are, too. If their basic needs are not met in a timely manner, and if they are cold, hungry, or isolated, they begin to feel that this is a world they cannot trust, that they are only sometimes safe. Inevitably, self blame commences as they begin to wonder if they are provoking this inconsistent response. The verbal and nonverbal messages that children receive from their parents or family, and what they understand these messages to mean are the foundations of the development of self.

During the first and early second years of life, the toddler's primary developmental task is to conquer the physical world. You can see these children bouncing off of corners, turning backwards, getting up, and walking off again. This active exploration also allows them to separate themselves from others. Their task is dealing with the issue, "Who am I, and how do you know I am me?" How can we provide any child, but especially the child of color, with an environment for explorations which say to them, "You are important at this early age"? It is never too soon to get that message across to the infant and toddler.

For the two- to five-year-old, growth is spurting. They are testing their world through language, actively exploring, feeling, seeking freedom, and wanting to make independent choices, whether they are ready to do so or not. All too often, they begin to feel that their needs for freedom are being impinged upon, and if they are stifled at a time when freedom of choice is important, they will begin to think, "What is it with this world?" Their needs to explore are great. But during this period, they need positive guidance and some protection toward developing self-control, as well as a sense of space for the building of autonomy. This requires a delicate balance for best results.

About this same time, children are beginning to experience their first steps toward the outside world. A big change in self perception occurs, as we saw with my children in nursery school. For many children today, their steps toward the bigger world occur even earlier. It is not unusual for an infant to enter child care at six weeks of age, or around the time when some mothers return to work after maternity leave. It has been well documented that many children of color feel positive about themselves when nestled within the comfort of their families, but when they get to preschool or kindergarten their self-image may be negatively affected, depending on these new experiences. Classmates begin to notice differences, and many children are viewed as novelties because of their color.

During the preschool years, children begin to understand cognitively what it is to be themselves and to explore the concepts of same and different. One important task centers around the measurement of their understanding of their cognitive skills by asking how things are different in size, shape, and color. This is often when a child asks another child, "Why are you brown?" or "Why is your hair curly?" or "Why aren't you like me?" Unfortunately, adults often clam up at these questions, and miss what could, in actuality, be a very teachable moment.

From the ages of approximately five to eight, children continue to grow physically. Independence persists as they build competencies in academic, social, and personal arenas. How well they do in school will, in large part, determine how they will feel about themselves. Conversely, they will also feel a certain way about themselves based on how well they do in school and the messages they receive about their adequacy. It is at this point when their cognition and their interests are being challenged on a daily basis at school.

At about the age of eight there is a cognitive shift and children begin preferring to be with others most like themselves. Belonging to a group becomes paramount. Boys prefer to be with boys and girls to be with girls. Social relationships take on a new meaning. Many children begin to prefer being with their own racial/ethnic groups for bonding and security.

From the years of eight to eleven, the child is refining many skills. Much testing and retesting takes place, and issues of morality surface as children ask, "Am I adequate? Am I a good person? Is it all right for them to be the way they are? Is it all right for me to be the way I am?" Between eight and eleven years, much energy is going into refining personal, physical, and academic skills as they continue to identify personal preferences which may include or exclude peers who are different.

From eleven to fourteen, there are many rapid changes as adolescence hits with force. Adolescence is a time of very serious work in terms of self-identity and self-worth. During that period, developmental tasks have to do with sexual identification, peer acceptance, and a need for privacy. Self-esteem during these years may appear to be on a roller coaster—high one day and low the next. Eventually, some stability begins to emerge. It doesn't always stay, but it does make an appearance. It is during this period that an attachment to a few close friends occurs. It is also a period in which peer pressure is so strong that children of varying racial/ethnic grounds who grew up together, even in similar socioeconomic groups, begin to drift away from each other, especially in social situations. These can be painful years for those who feel abandoned by life-long friends, but important ones in the development of self-esteem.

Thus, from a developmental point of view and perspective, we can glean the common human developmental stages through which children and young adolescents pass. We can also see junctures where children of color may be more vulnerable than others. Understanding and knowing that these stages exist is important in dealing with children and providing developmentally appropriate experiences and support.

Now let's address the issue of the importance of multicultural literature.

Why is it important to have multicultural literature? Donna Norton explains that

> [Multicultural literature is important because we are able to] gain [an] aesthetic appreciation as . . . [we] learn to understand and respect the artistic contributions of people from many cultural backgrounds. Multicultural literature helps . . . [children and youth] expand their

understanding of geography and natural history [and] increase their understanding of historical and sociological change . . .

Through carefully selected and shared literature, students learn to understand and to appreciate a literary heritage that comes from many diverse backgrounds. Through this literature, students learn to identify with people who created the stories . . . . From the past, they discover folktales, fables, myths, and legends that clarify the values and beliefs of the people . . . From the present, they discover the threads that weave the past with the present and the themes and values that continue to be important to the people.[11]

She continues to make a critical point about the personal importance to the reader by saying,

Of equal value are the personal gains acquired by students when they read great works from their own cultural background . . . They develop social sensitivity to the needs of others and realize that people have similarities as well as differences.[12]

Norton concludes that:

Developing understanding of our literary heritage, whether it is European, African, Native American, Hispanic or Asian, is one of the most important tasks facing educators . . . . Multicultural literature broadens . . . [children's] appreciation for literary techniques used by authors from different cultural backgrounds . . . . [It] improves their reading, writing, and thinking abilities.[13]

Multicultural literature is important in all settings. It must be available for purchase for our homes where it will be available to the entire family. Generations of people have never had the advantage of reading authentic multicultural literature by and about people of color because there has not been a great deal available until recently. Remember that there was not much out there for you or for me. We have to produce it, find it, purchase it, have it in our homes, have it available in our libraries, and have it as an integral part of our school curriculum now.

Many of the schools in which I am working have done a good job of purchasing multicultural literature for media centers and classroom use. I had an opportunity to talk to a white parent who had been at her child's school and had availed herself of looking at some of the multicultural literature in the library. This mother was fascinated. Her child brought home one of the books and they read it together. The mother said to me, "You know, I never knew those books were there. I am going to purchase these kinds of books for my children for Christmas." Two generations now know the power of this literature.

James Banks, in his book, *Multicultural Education, Issues and Perspectives*, speaks eloquently of the issue of self-esteem and its relationship to multicultural literature and multiethnic education. What some of us call "anglocentric education" he refers to as "mainstreamcentric curriculum." He believes that:

> A mainstreamcentric curriculum is one major way in which racism and ethnocentrism are reinforced and perpetuated in schools and society at large. This type of education has negative effects for mainstream students because it reinforces their false sense of superiority, gives them a misleading conception of their relationship with other racial and ethnic groups, and denies them the opportunity to benefit from the knowledge, perspective, and frames of references that can be gained from studying and experiencing other cultures and groups. When people view their culture from the perspective of another, they are able to understand their own culture more fully, and to see how it is unique and distinct from others as well as how it interrelates to and interacts with other cultures.[14]

When this happens, we begin to see a different reality.

We need to look for a balance in what is now an anglocentric curriculum. We are not talking about eliminating but balancing our curriculums with authentic literature and multicultural education across content areas, throughout the school year and throughout the entire span of our lives. James Banks believes that "absence of this approach damages children of color by marginalizing our experiences and our cultures. It does not reflect our dreams, our hopes, or our perspectives."[15]

Finally, what can we, as professionals, do?

1. We can make deliberate efforts to constantly challenge biases and prejudicial messages wherever they occur.

2. We must find, develop, purchase, and promote authentic multicultural literature.

3. We must find, nurture, and support children and youth of color who want to express themselves artistically. We must deliberately search for those with unrecognized potential and provide opportunities for them to express their gifts.

4. We must show that we do respect diversity by choosing to associate with people who are different from ourselves. Many of us work with people from different racial/ethnic backgrounds, but how many of us go to church with, or socialize with them? What you model for children, not only what you read to them, sends a direct message.

5. When children ask questions about differences, we must emphasize that differences are real, and they are not bad. Do not refuse to answer children's questions about hair, skin color, and other differences such as language and physical characteristics. A lack of response makes them feel there is something that cannot be discussed and, therefore, it must be bad. For children of color, it is a direct hit against positive self-esteem because it may mean to them that, "I do not exist, and, therefore I must be bad." In other words, encourage children and youth to openly discuss differences.

6. Take the time to read multicultural literature yourself. As you promote it to children and youth and adults, your excitement and enjoyment and validation of its importance will be evident and people will want to enjoy it because you do.

7. Promote literacy at all levels, and please, encourage children to read more and watch television less.

8. As children mature, discuss with them how stereotypes and prejudices are formed, and help them to recognize the insidious nature of these beliefs and how it affects perceptions and attitudes. In my present position, I have had many opportunities to talk with the middle and high school youngsters in our school district. They have a lot they need and want to talk about, and they express themselves well. One thing students often say to me is, "I don't understand why adults don't understand what we're going through!" My response to them is, "Perhaps you have to be their teachers on these issues." Please listen.

9. Find people of color who will tell their story. The oral traditions of people of color are vivid and rich, and they must be shared and preserved. We have our stories, we have our personal experiences, and they are rich.

10. Celebrate the authors and illustrators of color who have provided so much richness to our lives. Find them and thank them for the difference they make.

Lastly, we have the responsibility to send all of our children out into the world well prepared to contribute in many ways and on many levels in a multicultural and pluralistic society. At birth, they take their first steps on the journey that will take them well past the year 2009, when our mythical children of color graduate from high school. We must send our children out prepared to make significant contributions, and we must send them out with high self-esteem and self-worth. This will only happen when children of color feel affirmed, feel that they belong, and when their locus of control becomes internalized to the degree that they are confident that they can succeed against the odds. Only then will they be able to support the development of positive self-esteem in others.

Adults, as well, must have positive self-esteem. We cannot promote its development in others if we do not have it ourselves.

In closing, I would like to recall the words of a song which I believe is very appropriate. When we love ourselves, we are then able to embrace others and support the quest for high self-esteem. So let's close by affirming ourselves. The song is entitled "The Greatest Love of All." The music is by Michael Masser, with words by Linda Creed and sung by Whitney Houston.

> *I believe the children are our future.*
> *Teach them well, and let them show the way.*
> *Show them all the beauty they possess inside.*
> *Give them a sense of pride. . . .*
>
> *Learning to love yourself*
> *It is the greatest love of all.*[16]

Notes:

1. Hughes, "Freedom" from *The Panther and the Lash* by Langston Hughes. Copyright 1967 by Arna Bontemps and George Houston Bass. Reprinted by permission of Alfred A. Knopf, Inc.
2. NEA Report, Hispanic Concerns, 7.
3. NEA Report, American Indian/Alaskan Native Concerns, 7.
4. Ibid., 15.
5. NEA Report, Asian & Pacific Islander Concerns, 7.
6. Satir, *Toward a State of Esteem*, 9.
7. Kagle, in "How to Make Yourself a Stronger Person," 99.
8. Spencer, *Beginnings*, 216-219.
9. Ibid., 218.
10. Sparks, *Teaching Young Children to Resist Bias*, [1].
11. Norton, "Teaching Multicultural Literature," 28-29.
12. Ibid., 28.
13. Ibid., 29.
14. Banks, *Multicultural Education*, 189-190.
15. Ibid., 190.
16. Creed, "Greatest Love of All." Copyright © 1977 by Gold Horizon Music Corp. A Division of Filmtrax Copyright Holdings Inc. and Golden Torch Music Corp., A Division of Filmtrax Copyright Holdings Inc. All Rights Reserved.

Works Cited:

And Justice for All: The NEA Executive Committee Study Group Reports on Ethnic Minority Concerns. (Contents: "Hispanic Concerns"; "American Indian/Alaskan Native Concerns"; "Asian & Pacific Islander Concerns"; "African-American Concerns") Washington, DC: National Education Association Publishers, 1987.

Banks, James A., and Cherry A. Banks. *Multicultural Education: Issues and Perspectives.* Boston: Allyn & Bacon, 1989.

Creed, Linda and Masser, Michael. "The Greatest Love of All." Gold Horizon Music Corp. A Division of Filmtrax Copyright Holdings Inc. and Golden Torch Music Corp., A Division of Filmtrax Copyright Holdings Inc., 1977.

Hughes, Langston. "Freedom" in *The Panther and the Lash.* New York: Alfred A. Knopf, Inc., 1967.

Kagle, Arlene, in "How to Make Yourself A Stronger Person," by Claire Berman. *Ladies Home Journal*, 11 (1990): 99.

Norton, Donna E. "Teaching Multicultural Literature in the Reading Curriculum." *The Reading Teacher*, 44, no. 1 (September, 1990): 28-40.

Satir, Virginia, in *Toward a State of Esteem: Final Report of the California Task Force to Promote Self-esteem and Personal and Social Responsibility*. California State Department of Education, (Jan, 1990): 9.

Sparks, L.D., M. Guitierrez, and B. Phillips. *"Teaching Young Children to Resist Bias: What Parents Can Do."* Washington, DC: NAEYC Publishing, [1989?]: No. 565.

Spencer, Margaret B., G.K. Brookings, and W. Allen, Editors. *Beginnings: The Social and Affective Development of Black Children*. New Jersey: Lawrence Erlbaum Associates, Publishers, 1987.

Selected Publications by Virginia Henderson:

Henderson, Virginia, committee chair. *Elementary Minority Student Achievement Report*. Madison, WI: Madison Metropolitan School District, 1988.

Henderson, Virginia, committee chair. *Secondary Minority Student Achievement Report*. Madison, WI: Madison Metropolitan School District, 1990.

Evaluating Books by and about African-Americans

Rudine Sims Bishop

"A people's story is the anchor dat keeps um from driftin, it's the compass to show the way to go and it's a sail dat holds the power dat take um forward."[1] Camille Yarbrough, in her recent book, *The Shimmershine Queens,* puts those words into the mouth of 90-year-old Cousin Seatta. Cousin Seatta is referring specifically to African-American history, but since that history is often passed on in the form of story, her statement speaks both to the power and the importance of story within a cultural group. To the extent that a people's story is encompassed in their literature, this metaphor also places the value of accuracy and authenticity in African-American children's literature in an appropriate context. It casts story as the foundation, the guide, and the motivation on the journey through life. Cousin Seatta's statement assumes that the primary, in the sense of the first but not necessarily the only, audience for a people's story is the people themselves. African-American literature for African-American children is primary, but it is also true that the story of African-Americans is part of the story of America itself, and its proper audience is therefore everyone for whom the American story is important. As is the case with all literature, the quality of African-American literature varies, so my goal here is to discuss evaluating books about African-Americans, and specifically to focus on accuracy and authenticity.

Shadow and Substance is the title of a book about realistic fiction by and about African-Americans, published in 1982. It was the report of my survey and content analysis of 150 books about Blacks, published between 1965 and 1980. I will reexamine here some of the issues that were raised in that study in light of what has happened since 1980, to create a context for thinking about ways to evaluate African-American literature for accuracy and authenticity.

Rudine Sims Bishop is a Professor of Education at the Ohio State University. A graduate of West Chester University (PA), Professor Bishop also holds an M.Ed. from the University of Pennsylvania and an Ed.D. from Wayne State University in Detroit. She taught elementary school in Pennsylvania for a number of years, and was on the faculty of the University of Massachusetts. Ms. Bishop lives in Columbus, Ohio.

Three issues guided the analysis of the 150 books discussed in *Shadow and Substance*. The first issue was the implied reader for African-American literature, based on my assumption that an author's sense of whether she were writing about Black children for a primarily Black audience, or a primarily white audience, or both, would have an effect on both the content and the telling of the story. The second guiding issue was the tension between a view of the United States population as culturally homogeneous, and a view of the U.S. population as composed of varied and diverse and distinguishable parallel cultures. During the period that I was doing that analysis, "multicultural" was not the buzzword that it is today. "Color-blind" was considered to be the ideal, and celebrating difference was often considered divisive, at worst, and uncomfortable, at best. The tension between that attitude and the desire of many African-Americans to claim and celebrate a distinct Black culture was reflected in the kinds of books that were created at the time. In examining the books, I inferred their viewpoint by determining whether aspects of the culture were included in the literature or whether they were ignored. The third issue that guided the analysis was the cultural perspective from which the book was written, the base from which the author viewed his or her subjects. Did the book reflect an insider's view of Black life and culture, or an outsider's one? It may be that the first and second issues on some level were actually aspects of the third, which is, in my view, still the most relevant for today.

In any case, the three guiding questions served to divide those 150 books into three categories which I labeled **social conscience**, **melting pot**, and **culturally conscious**. Those categories formed a framework within which I could examine the distinguishing characteristics, both negative and positive, of books about Blacks, and from that imply a set of criteria for examining similar books. Will that framework still work as a way to look at books about African-Americans today?

The first category, **social conscience**, parts of which could be labeled "Guess Who's Coming to Dinner" books, was a reflection of the times. As far as I can tell, few books of this variety are being published today, and many of those discussed in *Shadow and Substance* are out-of-print and hard to get—a blessing, for the most part. Today's framework would either have to exclude those books or relegate them to a discussion of the history of African-American children's literature prior to 1970. The other two categories are still with us, although many of the specific books included in the *Shadow and Substance* survey are now out-of-print.

The **melting pot** category could profitably be reexamined. I revisited that chapter recently, and I was reminded of something that has often been lost in discussions of that analysis, which tend to center on just one subcategory of the melting pot books. At least half of the books examined at that time were focused on racial integration, and thus were the likely basis for the melting pot category. About 25 percent of those books were told from the point of view of white children, the "me-and-my-Black-friend" books; I don't know that there are many of those books coming out today. Another 30 percent of the melting pot books were racially integrated. They had Black children as main characters but those children were in integrated settings and outside of the family circle. The other half, the ones most often discussed, which included several of the Ezra Jack Keats' "Peter" books, such as *The Snowy Day* and *Peter's Chair*, focused on Black children in the context of their families and their neighborhood.

Those are the books that most resemble the third category, culturally conscious, and most resemble some of the current crop of books. This is the group that I had the most difficult time fitting into one of the three categories. Earlier I mentioned that one of the features distinguishing those books from the melting pot books was that nothing in the text indicated the culture or the race of the characters. Another decade of experience with picture books suggests that were I to do it today, I would examine the illustrations even more closely than I did the first time. Illustrations are an essential part of the telling of a picture book story, and it may be that the pictures contained some motifs, elements, or stylistic markers that would place them in a third category.

The third category, **culturally conscious**, is still going strong. Those are the books that placed major Black characters within the context of Black families and neighborhoods, the story was told from their perspective, and something in the text, as well as the pictures, indicated that this was a story about a Black child. It is advisable to remember, however, that this category was not labeled culturally authentic, a deliberate choice because, although all the books in the category were judged to indicate an awareness of Black culture, they were not all judged to be either accurate or authentic in the handling of it. About 73 percent of the culturally conscious books were written by Black authors, and about 40 percent of those by just five writers. Those were the books that I claimed could be considered the core of the body of modern African-American children's literature. That tradition is still very much with us, and today's framework would be dominated by such books.

I have noted that I am not certain whether the framework that worked for the original *Shadow and Substance* is still entirely useful to maintain in looking at today's books about African-Americans. That is not to suggest that the framework was wrong, simply that we need to remember that the categories were derived from an examination of a specific set of 150 books of realistic fiction, published between 1965 and 1979. Current books differ from those, and the framework would need adjusting to accommodate them. The survey was also limited to contemporary realistic fiction, and while that genre still dominates African-American children's literature, other kinds of literature should be considered as well.

When we think about what is available today and what kinds of books by and about African-Americans we are interested in knowing how to evaluate, we must consider some publishing statistics. Of 5,000 children's books published in 1990, about one percent were written by African-American authors. Even adding non-Black authors writing about African-Americans will not increase that number substantially. Over the past few years, the total percentage of books published each year featuring African-Americans has been hovering somewhere between one and two percent. My impression is that within that one and two percent we have seen an important increase in picture books and a concomitant decrease in the number of novels. We have seen a focus on African-American folklore and folk-like stories, such as those of Patricia McKissack (*Flossie and the Fox* and *Nettie Jo's Friends*), and we've seen an increase in the quality, but not the quantity, of nonfiction.

An important recent trend shows that, unlike the 1970s, most of the books about African-Americans currently being published are written and/or illustrated by African-Americans. There are exceptions, and most of the criticisms and controversies related to African-American children's literature swirl around those exceptions. Controversies arise because the long, sad history of U.S. race relations, coupled with the tradition of negative images of Blacks presented in children's books, make African-American readers and other knowledgeable critics sensitive to even the most subtle manifestations of racism, negative attitudes, and prejudices.

Unfortunately, such attitudes and prejudices are so much a part of the fabric of life in this country that they can be held even by people whose basic intentions are good. Newspapers from time to time report surveys that show a majority of white Americans believing that Blacks are less intelligent, more violence prone than they are, etc. Such attitudes influence who gets jobs and the kinds of jobs they get, who lives in substandard housing, who gets good or poor medical care, and—most important to many of us—the quality of education offered to people for whom education is the "hope factor," the way to a better life. When controversy erupts over the images in children's books, protests have to be understood as part of the larger social and cultural context of which the books are a part. That is why the little flier, "Ten Quick Ways to Analyze Children's Books for Racism and Sexism," put out by the Council on Interracial Books for Children is still relevant today. A more general discussion of criteria for literature about people of color can be found in Masha Rudman's book, *Children's Literature: An Issues Approach*.

But what I want to focus on is the idea that one way to understand what is authentic African-American children's fiction is to become familiar with the body of work that exists. I want to urge you to think not so much of "evaluation," as to think of celebration and appreciation. If you want authentic African-American experience, go to the people who have lived it and who bring those life experiences to bear on creating literature for children. Read Walter Dean Myers, Eloise Greenfield, Virginia Hamilton, Patricia McKissack, Mildred Pitts Walter, Joyce Hansen, and Elizabeth Fitzgerald Howard. Look closely at the visual work of Tom Feelings, John Steptoe, Jerry Pinkney, and Pat Cummings. When you have immersed yourself in their work, you will have some basis for comparison as you meet new books and new writers, and writers whose perspective is not African-American.

When you find their work, what kinds of things are you likely to find? What do Black writers and illustrators do that mark their work as coming out of an African-American experience? One of the first things you will notice is variety. An anthropologist colleague tells me that within any culture there is more difference than there is similarity. One kind of difference is likely to be in the quality of the writing. Expect variety in literary quality and accept it. On the other hand, merely including African-American experience is no excuse for poor literary quality. Secondly, you will find variety in the portrayals of Blacks, because the African-American experience is not a monolith. Black people live in suburbs, Black people live in the country, we live in small towns as well as the city. Growing up Black in a small coal-mining town in Pennsylvania is no less an African-American experience than growing up in Harlem. It is a different one in some ways, but it is similar as well. Variety will also be found in socioeconomic levels. There are African-American lawyers, and doctors, and professors, as well as people who are homeless and people who are financially poor.

One recently published authentic African-American picture book demonstrates some of the shared values to be found in such literature. It is Elizabeth Fitzgerald Howard's *Aunt Flossie's Hats (and Crab Cakes Later)*, a first person narrative that tells the story of two sisters who spend their Sunday afternoons with their great-great aunt. Aunt Flossie has an old house "crowded full of stuff and things,"[2] including "boxes and boxes and boxes of HATS!"[3] After tea and cookies, Aunt Flossie lets the girls get at the hatboxes. "We pick out hats and try them on. Aunt Flossie says they are her memories, and each hat has its own story."[4] As the girls try on hats, Aunt Flossie tells the stories they evoke. After the hats and stories, Aunt Flossie, the girls, and the girls' parents go out for crab cakes. "Nothing in the whole wide world tastes as good as crab cakes. But crab cakes taste better after stories . . . stories about Aunt Flossie's hats!"[5]

Contrary to the expectations of many that African-American literature must be about low-income city dwellers or Blacks fighting racism or discrimination, *Aunt Flossie's Hats* features a middle or upper middle class Black family. These are people who are what some would call "drylongso" human beings. The epigraph to John Langston Gwaltney's book by that title quotes Harriet Jones, a pseudonymous teenager:

Since I don't see myself or most people I know in most things I see or read about black people, I can't be bothered with that. I wish you could read something or see a movie that would show the people just, well, as my grandmother would say, drylongso. You know, like most of us really are most of the time — together enough to do what we have to do to be decent people.[6]

Aunt Flossie's Hats does just that.

The language of *Aunt Flossie's Hats* is standard English. Other writers, given their settings and characters, use different language patterns. For example, Walter Dean Myers is superb at creating the language of modern day African-American young men in the city:

> *Ka-phoomp! Ka-phoomp! Da Doom Da Doom!*
> *Ka-phoomp! Ka-phoomp! Da Doom Da Doom!*
> *You can call me Mouse, 'cause that's my tag*
> *I'm into it all, everything's my bag*
> *You know I can run, you know I can hoop*
> *I can do it alone, or in a group [. . .]*[7]

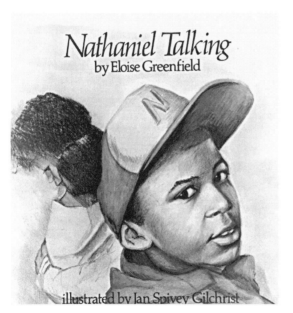

From Nathaniel Talking by Eloise Greenfield. Copyright © 1988 by Eloise Greenfiled, illustrations by Jan Spivey Gilchrist. Reprinted by permission of Black Butterfly.

Lucille Clifton, on the other hand, creates the informal vernacular of an eight-year-old African-American girl:

> My brother Baggy, he gonna run away. He say he tired of Mama and Daddy always telling him what to do. He say he a Black man, a warrior. And he can make it by hisself. So he gonna run away. I help him get his stuff together.[8]

African-American writers are also influenced by African-American music. If you read Eloise Greenfield's poetry, for example, you can find the language and rhythm of the blues:

> *my daddy sings the blues*
> *he plays it on his old guitar*
> *my daddy sings the blues*
> *he plays it on his old guitar [. . .]*[9]

My point is that the language of *Aunt Flossie's Hats* is one of a number of varieties of language patterns used by African-Americans, and that authentic African-American literature uses language appropriate to the time, place, circumstances, age, and educational level of the characters and the story.

Aunt Flossie's Hats exemplifies another value found often in African-American children's literature: celebration of family. Many such books feature warm, respectful, and loving relationships between youngsters and their elderly relatives. They celebrate, not just the nuclear family, but the extended family as well. Older relatives include those other than grandparents. Aunt Flossie is a great-great aunt. In Sharon Bell Mathis's *The Hundred Penny Box*, the elderly relative is one hundred-year-old Aunt Dewbet Thomas. In some books, such as

Eloise Greenfield's *Grandpa's Face* and Valerie Flournoy's *The Patchwork Quilt*, the older relatives are living with the family, as active, valued contributors to the lives of the children. In other books, children are being raised by their grandparents, a reflection of a historical reality that continues today for many families.

Often these books incorporate some aspect of African-American history and heritage—heroes and sheroes. When Eloise Greenfield collected a set of poems about love, she included Harriet Tubman, who ". . . didn't take no stuff / Wasn't

From Shake It to the One that You Love the Best: Play Songs and Lullabies from Black Musical Traditions. Copyright© 1989 by Warren-Mattox Productions. Reprinted by permission of Warren-Mattox Productions.

scared of nothing neither."[10] In *Justin and the Best Biscuits in the World*, Mildred Pitts Walter included a passage in which the grandfather, who has taken his grandson away to help him to grow up a little bit and teach him something about being a Black man within that family, takes the time to tell the child the history of African-Americans who were homesteaders and about the kinds of problems they had to solve to survive. In *The Black Snowman*, there is a celebration of African heritage and kente cloth. The magic of that African heritage helps a young boy come to grips with who he is. Sometimes African-American history and heritage is central to the book. Joyce Hansen's books, *Which Way Freedom?* and *Out from this Place*, present an African-American perspective on the Civil War and its aftermath. *Shake*

It to the One that You Love the Best, a collection of play songs and lullabies, is a celebration of African-American culture, music, and art. In *Aunt Flossie's Hats*, the illustrations of the big parade in Baltimore show some of the returning soldiers as belonging to the 92nd Division. The artist was celebrating some African-American history: Black participation in World War I.

Another value important to African-American children's literature is the notion of pride and identity. In Cheryl and Wade Hudson's *Bright Eyes, Brown Skin*, this pride is the primary focus of the book. Pride and identity are also central in *The Shimmershine Queens*, from which I took my opening quote.

In the writing of many African-American authors there is a sense of community, in which community is defined as the family of African-American people; there is a "we-ness." Sometimes the community is a neighborhood, as in *The Gold Cadillac*. When the father in that book buys a car the family celebrates, and the whole community celebrates with them, and then tries to talk him out of going to Mississippi in that gold cadillac in 1950. The whole community is concerned when they come back and start driving an old Ford. In Mildred Pitts Walter's book, *Because We Are*, the whole of the title proverb is, "Because We Are I Am," and the author's emphasis is on that sense of community. When Mirandy, in *Mirandy and Brother Wind*, wants to know how to capture the wind she not only goes to her family, she goes to the community.

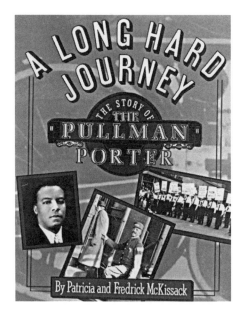

From *A Long Hard Journey*. Copyright © 1989 by Patricia and Fredrick McKissack. Reprinted by permission of Walker & Co.

Bernard Bell, a professor at the University of Massachusetts at Amherst, analyzed African-American novels for their thematic, stylistic, and structural characteristics. He asserts that the one theme shared across those books is a sense of survival, not only physical survival but psychological survival. That theme can be found in Walter Dean Myer's books, Virginia Hamilton's books, and in the works of many other African-American writers. These authors are trying to tell young African-American children, "You can survive. We have done it, we have come through a great deal, and we have survived." The family in *The Gold Cadillac* survives by maintaining their dignity in the face of racism. In *M. C. Higgins, the Great* a more physical kind of survival is demonstrated, but it is M. C. who must come to the realization that he is responsible, at least in part, for his own survival. Survival often is a theme in biographies, particularly those written by African-Americans, because the authors chose the perspective from which to view the people. Patricia and Fred McKissack, for example, recently published the story of the Pullman Porter. The McKissacks chose heroes who looked as if they were doing menial tasks, and on some level they were, but they help us to understand how the porters survived, how they maintained their dignity, and their sense of themselves.

We must not forget to examine the visual images in children's literature for accuracy and authenticity. When African-American artists illustrate books about African-Americans, they create attractive, realistic, recognizably African-American children. Examining how little Black girls wear their hair in illustrations is a worthwhile exercise. It is important that the artists show attractive braids and neatly combed hair. Dolls are another enlightening item to track. In the original edition of *What Mary Jo Shared*, a Raggedy Ann doll is sitting on Mary Jo's bed. Nothing is inherently wrong with Raggedy Ann dolls, but when African-American artists give dolls to little African-American girls, they are African-American dolls; they are reflections of themselves. These are small details, but they carry a message to the child reader.

Illustrations of crowd scenes are also revealing images to inspect. In both of the crowd scenes in *Aunt Flossie's Hats*, African-Americans predominate. You see African-American fire fighters, African-American soldiers, African-American waitresses, and African-Americans having dinner at a nice restaurant. It is important to African-American artists to show African-Americans in many and diverse ways.

I want to conclude by sharing another recently published book. It's called *Tar Beach*, and was created by Faith Ringgold from a story quilt she had made earlier, incorporating scenes from her early life in New York City. Tar Beach is the rooftop of the apartment building. The story begins this way.

> I will always remember when the stars fell down around me and lifted me up above the George Washington Bridge. I could see our tiny rooftop, with Mommy and Daddy and Mr. and Mrs. Honey, our next-door neighbors, still playing cards as if nothing was going on, and Be Be, my baby brother, lying real still on the mattress, just like I told him to, his eyes like huge floodlights tracking me through the sky. Sleeping on Tar Beach was magical. Lying on the roof at night, with stars and skyscraper buildings all around me, made me feel rich, like I owned all that I could see. The bridge was my most prized possession.[11]

The speaker is Cassie Louise Lightfoot, who is eight years old, and can fly. She understands that her imagination can set her free, and that she therefore can "go wherever I want for the rest of my life."[12]

Tar Beach, too, exemplifies some important aspects of African-American culture as presented in books for children. Its genesis as a quilt is a reminder of an aspect of the artistic heritage of African-Americans that receives too little attention. And in her imaginary journeys Cassie remembers the racial discrimination that has kept her father from making full use of his talents and skills, a condition faced by generations of African-Americans. She vows to make a difference, and expresses the confidence that she can because she can fly. "[. . .] Anyone can fly. All you need is somewhere to go that you can't get to any other way. The next thing you know, you're flying among the stars."[13]

From Tar Beach by Faith Ringgold. Copyright © 1991 by Faith Ringgold. Reprinted by permission of Crown Publishers, Inc.

Tar Beach and *Aunt Flossie's Hats* are just two examples of authentic African-American literatures available today. Careful examination of such books can provide serious, sensitive readers with a standard against which to judge the accuracy and authenticity of stories claiming to represent an African-American cultural perspective. Questions about accuracy and authenticity are important because the African-American story is a part of the story of this nation, and as Aunt Seatta reminded us, "A people's story is the anchor dat keeps um from driftin, it's the compass to show the way to go and it's a sail dat holds the power dat take um forward."[14] I wish you smooth sailing.

Notes:

1. Yarbrough, *Shimmershine Queens*, 21.
2. Howard, *Aunt Flossie's Hats*, 4.
3. Ibid., 5.
4. Ibid., 9.
5. Ibid., 30-31.
6. Gwaltney, *Drylongso*, xix.
7. Myers, *Mouse Rap*, 3.
8. Clifton, *My Brother Fine with Me*, 4.
9. Greenfield, *Nathaniel Talking*, 18.
10. Greenfield, *Honey, I Love*, 37.
11. Ringgold, *Tar Beach*, 3-7.
12. Ibid., 11.
13. Ibid., 25.
14. Yarbrough, *Shimmershine Queens*, 21.

Works Cited:

Bell, Bernard. *The Afro-American Novel and Its Tradition*. Amherst: University of Massachusetts Press, 1987.

Clifton, Lucille. *My Brother Fine with Me*. Illustrated by Moneta Barnett. New York: Holt, Rinehart and Winston, 1975.

Council on Interracial Books for Children. "Ten Quick Ways to Analyze Children's Books for Racism and Sexism," in *Guidelines for Selecting Bias Free Textbooks and Story Books*. New York: Council on Interracial Books for Children, [1984], pp. 24-26.

Flournoy, Valerie. *The Patchwork Quilt*. Illustrated by Jerry Pinkney. New York: Dutton, 1985.

Greenfield, Eloise. *Grandpa's Face*. Illustrated by Floyd Cooper. New York: Philomel, 1988.

———. *Honey, I Love and Other Love Poems*. Illustrated by Diane and Leo Dillon. New York: Thomas Y. Crowell, 1978.

———. *Nathaniel Talking*. Illustrated by Jan Spivey Gilchrist. New York: Black Butterfly, 1988.

Gwaltney, John Langston. *Drylongso: A Self Portrait of Black America*. New York: Random House, 1980.

Hamilton, Virginia. *M. C. Higgins, the Great*. New York: Macmillan, 1974.

Hansen, Joyce. *Out from this Place*. New York: Walker, 1986.

———. *Which Way Freedom?* New York: Walker, 1986.

Howard, Elizabeth Fitzgerald. *Aunt Flossie's Hats (and Crab Cakes Later)*. Illustrated by James Ransome. New York: Clarion, 1991.

Hudson, Cheryl. *Bright Eyes, Brown Skin*. Illustrated by George Ford. Orange, NJ: Just Us Books, 1990.

Keats, Ezra Jack. *The Snowy Day*. New York: Viking, 1962.

———. *Peter's Chair*. New York: Harper & Row, 1967.

Mathis, Sharon Bell. *The Hundred Penny Box*. Illustrated by Leo and Diane Dillon. New York: Viking, 1975.

Mattox, Cheryl Warren, comp. *Shake It to the One that You Love the Best: Play Songs and Lullabies from Black Musical Traditions*. Illustrated by Varnette P. Honeywood and Brenda Joysmith. El Sobrante, Cal.: Warren-Mattox Productions, 1989.

McKissack, Patricia. *Flossie and the Fox*. Illustrated by Rachel Isadora. New York: Dial, 1986.

———. *and Brother Wind*. Illustrated by Jerry Pinkney. New York: Knopf, 1988.

———. *Nettie Jo's Friends*. Illustrated by Scott Cook. New York: Knopf, 1989.

McKissack, Patricia, and Fredrick McKissack. *A Long Hard Journey: The Story of the Pullman Porter*. New York: Walker, 1989.

Mendez, Phil. *The Black Snowman*. Illustrated by Carole Byard. New York: Scholastic, 1989.

Myers, Walter Dean. *The Mouse Rap*. New York: Harper & Row, 1990.

Ringgold, Faith. *Tar Beach*. New York: Crown, 1991.

Rudman, Masha. *Children's Literature: An Issues Approach*. 2d ed. White Plains, NY: Longman, 1984, pp. 162-166.

Sims, Rudine. *Shadow and Substance: Afro-American Experience in Contemporary Children's Fiction*. Urbana, Ill.: National Council of Teachers of English, 1982.

Taylor, Mildred D. *The Gold Cadillac*. Illustrated by Michael Hays. New York: Dial, 1987.

Udry, Janice May. *What Mary Jo Shared*. Illustrated by Eleanor Mill. Chicago: Whitman, 1966.

Walter, Mildred Pitts. *Because We Are*. New York: Lothrop, 1983.

———. *Justin and the Best Biscuits in the World*. Illustrated by Catherine Stock. New York: Lothrop, 1986.

Yarbrough, Camille. *The Shimmershine Queens*. New York: G. P. Putnam's Sons, 1989.

Selected Works by Rudine Sims Bishop

Books:

Presenting Walter Dean Myers. (Volume in Twayne's American Authors Series of Bio-critical Books) Boston: Twayne Publications/G.K. Hall, 1990.

Shadow and Substance: Afro-American Experience in Contemporary Children's Fiction. Urbana, Ill.: National Council of Teachers of English, 1982.

Articles and Chapters:

"Children's Books in a Multicultural World: The View from the U.S." *Reading against Racism*. Ed. by W.D. Emrys. London: Open University Press. In Press.

"The Treatment of Literature and Minorities in *Becoming a Nation of Readers*." *Counterpoint and Beyond: A Response to Becoming a Nation of Readers*. Ed. by Jane Davidson. Urbana, Ill.: National Council of Teachers of English, 1988.

"Extending Multicultural Understanding through Children's Books." *Children's Literature in the Reading Program*. Ed. by Bernice Cullinan. Newark, Del.: International Reading Association, 1987.

"Children's Books about Blacks: A Mid-Eighties Status Report." Guest Essay. *Children's Literature Review*, Vol. 8. Detroit: Gale Research, 1985.

"A Question of Perspective, III." *The Advocate*, 4, no. 2 (Winter 1985): final page, not numbered.

"Strong Black Girls: A Ten Year Old Response to Fiction About Afro-Americans." *Journal of Research and Development in Education*, 16, no. 3 (Spring 1983): 21-28.

"What Has Happened to the 'All-White' World of Children's Books?" *Phi Delta Kappan*, 64, no. 9 (May 1983): 650-653.

"Dialect and Reading: Toward Redefining the Issues." *Reader Meets Author/Bridging the Gap: A Psycholinguistic and Sociolinguistic Perspective*. Edited by Judith Langer and Margaret Smith-Burke. Newark, Del.: International Reading Association, 1982.

"Profile: A Conversation with Lucille Clifton." *Language Arts*, 59, no. 2 (February 1982): 160-167. Reprinted in *Children's Literature Review*, 5. Detroit: Gale Research, 1983.

"Children's Literature and Black Women: Images and Authors." *New England Journal of Black Studies*. (Spring 1981).

"What We Know about Dialects and Reading." *Findings in Research in Reading Miscue Analysis: Classroom Implications*. Ed. by P. David Allen and Dorothy J. Watson. Urbana, Ill.: National Council of Teachers of English, 1976.

"Black Children and the Language Arts: A Call for Reform." *Ebonics: The True Language of Black Folk*. Ed. by Robert L. Williams and Alvin Goins. St. Louis: Institute for Black Studies, 1975.

With Goodman, Yetta. "Whose Dialect for Beginning Readers?" *Elementary English* 51 (September 1984): 837-841. Reprinted in *What's New in Reading*. Ed. by Iris Tiedt. Urbana, Ill.: National Council of Teachers of English, 1974.

Reviews:

"Words by Heart: A Black Perspective." Review of *Words by Heart* by Ouida Sebestyen. *Interracial Books for Children Bulletin*, 11, no. 7 (1980): 12-15, 17.

Transcending the Form
Tom Feelings

Playwright August Wilson, two-time winner of the Pulitzer Prize, took on Hollywood in 1990. In an article entitled, "I Don't Want to Hire Nobody Just 'Cause They're Black," he was quoted as saying, "Fight racism by respecting African-American culture, not by denying it."[1] Mr. Wilson goes on to describe his struggle with Hollywood to hire a Black director for his play. He found a "prevailing attitude . . . that a Black director couldn't do the job and to insist upon one is to make the film 'unmakeable.'"[2] About a well-known, highly respected white director who expressed interest in the project, Wilson said,

> He is not Black. He is not a product of black-American culture—a culture that was honed out of the black experience and fired in the kiln of slavery and survival—and he does not share the sensibilities of black Americans. I have been asked if I am not, by rejecting him on the basis of his race, doing the same thing Paramount Pictures is doing by not hiring a black director . . . . I am trying to get the film of my play made in the best possible way. As Americans of various races we share a broad cultural ground, a commonality of society that links its various and diverse elements into a cohesive whole that can be defined as "American" . . . . We share . . . history . . . [and] political and economic systems, and a rapidly developing, if suspect, ethos. Within these commonalities are specifics. Specific ideas and attitudes that are not shared on the common cultural ground. These remain the property and possession of the people who developed them . . . . Someone who does not share the specifics of a culture remains an outsider, no matter how astute a student they are or how well-meaning their intentions."[3]

Tom Feelings is an artist and illustrator of books for children and young teenagers. Born and raised in Brooklyn, New York, he studied at the School of Visual Arts in New York City. In 1964, He was invited by the Government of Ghana to live there and work as an illustrator for the Ghanian Government Publishing House in Accra. Between 1971 and 1974, he lived in Guyana, South America, where he provided opportunities for young artists to create illustrations for a national textbook program in which instructional materials for children were to become relevant to their own life and history. Recognition for his illustrations includes a Coretta Scott King Book Award for Illustration, two Caldecott Honor Book distinctions, and a Boston Globe - Horn Book Award for Illustration. Mr. Feelings is a member of the art department at the University of South Carolina.

References are cited in the text to illustrations which could not be included in this book. - Ed.

August Wilson's sentiments are just as pertinent to children's book publishing as they are to the film industry. Truly authentic multicultural books are created—written *and* illustrated—by people who belong to the race, culture or nation of origin which is reflected in the book. The easiest way to see the truth in this is by examining the books themselves, and particularly by comparing work done by people of a culture which matches that of the book with that done by people outside of it.

I wasn't getting what I needed in my illustration class so I went out on the streets of Brooklyn and started drawing. The assignments had nothing to do with Black people. So finally I decided to draw those things and those people I had seen all my life. I went out in the streets with a pad and started drawing.

To get to what *was*, to what *will be*, you must go through what *is*. Lorraine Hansberry said that naturalism tends to take the world as it is.[4] This is what it is. This is how it happened. This is true because we see it everyday in life. It is a photographic process. In realism, the artist who is creating the realistic work imposes on it not only what it *is* but what is *possible*. This is part of a reality, too. It allows a much larger potential for what human beings can do. It requires much greater selectivity. You don't just put down everything you've seen, you put down what you believe *is*. Realism demands the imposition of a point of view.

When I couldn't get work dealing with Black people and was told that my focus on drawing and painting Black people was limiting my scope, and because I wanted to find out more about myself, I went to Ghana. The pictures I did when I was in Ghana were "realistic"—and very different from my previous work.

When I came back from Africa, I continued drawing my community: Bedford-Stuyvesant in Brooklyn, New York, on a Saturday afternoon. Because of the experience of living in Africa, because of being in the majority for the first time in my life, because of being surrounded by Black people, because of realizing the thing that John Henrik Clarke calls, in Africa, a constant Celebration of Life and Death, there is more movement in my work. I'm being more than a reporter. I have a point of view. This is what I brought back and tried to show in the books that I did after returning from Africa.

When I talk about culture, I'm talking about a point of view. The things that come out of Black culture are part of what John Henrik Clarke called "improvising within a restricted view." As a metaphor, I would call Black peoples' journey to America and our constant struggle for freedom here, improvising within a restrictive form and transcending the form.

If you listen to Black music, you are aware of it. When Miles Davis plays some corny tune, like "Some Day My Prince Will Come" straight, and then plays it again so that you hear new things, he's transcended the form and made it almost a new

Bed Sty on a Saturday Afternoon (Brooklyn, New York). Copyright © Tom Feelings.

song. Mohammed Ali took boxing beyond the form, beyond what was done before. It's not enough for Black basketball players just to put the ball in the hoop and just win the game. They jump up in the air, twist, turn, soar, then dunk it. It transcends the form. You will see some of this in Black artists' work.

Rachel Isadora is a good artist. I like her work. But I can't remember the last time I went into a Black home, no matter how poor, where the grandmother and the mother would let a child stand up on the couch with his shoes on, as she shows in *Ben's Trumpet* (p. 18-19). That is a cultural difference and insensibility.

I have heard Black people say that they wish they were everything, in terms of being free, and they wish they could fly. But I have never heard them say that they wish they was a buzzard as the book *Oh Lord, I Wish I Was a Buzzard* implies. If you look at the face of the girl in *Oh Lord . . .* (cover) and then look at a drawing by Carole Byard, you can compare the difference. In a society that does not celebrate blackness or darkness, (as a matter of fact there are 90 negative connotations for the word "black" in the dictionary and of course, the exact opposite for the word "white"), Carole Byard makes her people as dark as she cares to. You still see the glow, you still see something about the face that goes beyond just form. It transcends the form.

In *Everett Anderson's Nine Month Long* (p. 2) or *Osa's Pride* (p. 31), illustrated by Ann Grifalconi, look at the lips, the shape of the head, the nose, the eyes, and the hair

Illustration by Carole Byard reprinted by permission of Philomel Books from Grandmama's Joy by Eloise Greenfield, illustrations copyright © 1980 by Carole Byard.

of her people. Graphically the profiles work, sometimes, but when you look into the center of the faces, the content doesn't hold together—not as Black people.

If you use pure design, art can get very cold. If you use too much realism it can get very syrupy. How do you balance these two? How do you get them to work together? In Africa, we don't believe that pain and joy sit side-by-side; rather, they interact, like life. In this society, people tend to think that sensitivity and softness belong to women while hardness and strength belong to men, and that the two opposites just sit there, unrelated. Often artwork done by African-Americans shows a combination of both these characteristics in one subject.

Jean Toomer, a Black writer, said that "an artist is he who can balance strong contrast, who can combine opposing forms and forces in significant unity." For me, a significant part of our Black heritage in America—and a driving force in my own work—is that constant combining and balancing of seemingly unequal forces.

George Ford's illustrations for the book by Eloise Greenfield on Paul Robeson embody those things normally considered opposites. Paul Robeson was a very strong physical individual. But there is almost a softness and a tenderness about these pictures in terms of his personality and who he is that encompasses these two things that I said sit side-by-side but also interact.

Look at the mother and child in Mozelle Thompson's *Lift Every Voice and Sing* (p. 14-15). In the few lines Thompson uses you can see that he knows what these faces look like, from outside the form and inside the content.

In *Shaka, King of the Zulus* by Diane Stanley, one sees a boy walking down an African road looking like a tired old man. But in Mozelle Thompson's art, one sees his design factor in terms of the light and dark and the shape of the head and the face; the body with all of the vital energy of a young boy moving and a style that incorporates a dance consciousness. It makes all the difference.

Catherine Stock had recently returned from Africa when she illustrated *Galimoto*. She truly wanted to do a book about African children, but the figures do not look real. In contrast, when you compare it to George Ford's work in *Walk On* and *The*

Best Time of Day, you find human beings, people you see on the street every day, alive, with energy. It's got to do with seeing and perception and living that life.

In Mozelle Thompson's *Pumpkinseeds,* now out of print, one notices how he enlarged the hands on purpose, working, once again, in black and white. Sometimes artists enlarge images to express ideas. Black artists frequently will do this to make a point. I was in a unbiased art show in 1976 where we were supposed to look at illustrations and pick out the things that had no bias in them. I was one

The Best Time of Day. Copyright © 1978 by Random House, Inc. Reprinted by permission of Random House, Inc.

of five judges, and the only Black judge. As we went through the work the other judges would set aside things that they did not want in the show, and I would put them back in. I'm talking about the Black things. I realized, because of our different experiences, things that they saw as distorted and raw, I saw as a part of the Black experience. It reminded me of listening to James Brown—you like the rhythm but the grunts and the screams that he makes bother you—so you'd rather hear Pat Boone sing the song making it easier on the ears. The difference is sensibility. Or more recently, the rappers: white rapper Vanilla Ice copies the form, it did not originate with him, but because his image is lighter on the eyes (pun intended), it can be accepted more readily in the mainstream.

Jacob Lawrence enlarged Harriet's hand for a reason in *Harriet and the Promised Land* (p. 15). Some people have complained that Harriet looks much older than her stated age of 14 because her hand is distorted. Jacob Lawrence is trying to say, with that distortion, that this is every Black woman who scrubbed a floor for nothing. That's what is portrayed in this picture. It was taken beyond the form, but the form balances with the content, and especially with the *story* being told.

It means a lot to Black mothers to braid their children's hair and they usually put a lot of work into the design of it. In Catherine Stock's illustrations for *Secret Valentine* the hair is not in a design. However, in *Cornrows* illustrated by Carole Byard you see the movement, the rhythm in the hair styles. Black art often exhibits a dance consciousness that is clearly in our culture. You hear it in the music, you see it in the dance. Black artists try to project it in their own form of art.

Jerry Pinkney's work offers many opportunities to see cultural authencity and also great linear movement. *Wild, Wild Sunflower Child Anna* is a good example.

Ezra Jack Keats book *The Snowy Day* was done in the early 1960s. It was the first time there was a focus on a Black character in a children's book. The book was beautifully done at that time and is very "design-y." I give him credit for that. But if you look at the profiles carefully, you will see all Keats had to do was take out that brown color, and he'd have a white child. If the form is not clear, how can the content ring true?

Almost 20 years later, James Ransome did a book with Angela Johnson, *Do Like Kyla*. He did something similar to Ezra Jack Keats, but he *combined* realism with design. The balance is there, the excitement of design. Design can be used as excitement but when you put real people in it, it makes the viewer identify with the human beings.

From *Do Like Kyla* by Angela Johnson. Illustration copyright © 1990 by James E. Ransome. Reprinted with permission of the publisher, Orchard Books.

Pat Cummings' work in *Just Us Women* (pp. 28-29) shows the different colors within the Black community. She interprets this in her illustration of the girl and her aunt, who are both light in color.

We Keep a Store (p. 17) is a people's story and it shows the relationships of a little girl and her mother and father, the storekeepers. The illustrations have a definite point of view. They are not photographs. Now, John Ward might have taken a photograph of the scene in preparation for his illustrative work, but he used design

Illustrations from Carole Byard by permission of Coward, McCann & Geohegan from Cornrows by Camille Yarbrough, illustrations copyright © 1979 by Carole Byard.

and realism to show you the warmth between the child, the father, and the mother within the picture.

Grandmama's Joy (pp. 31-32) is a story about a little girl who realizes that her grandmother works hard every day at a long, difficult job. When she comes home she's very tired. The little girl tells her grandmother all sorts of stories to cheer her up and she finally does. Carole Byard knows that people are turned off to anything that is all Black in this society because we are programmed to do that. Yet, she believes as an artist that she can take you past the program, especially those people who need it the most. And that's what you see in her faces. There's a glow in the faces. When you first look at it, you see beautiful form and design—but then she pulls you into the center of it by creating a mood for the audience to complete.

I'm trying to do the same thing, with a book on slavery. I want to do it all in black and white, and still make you feel the opposite of what you've been programmed to feel. Something that's all in black is supposed to be a negative, but I want you to feel that it is regal and open, sometimes. And the opposite as well: something that is all in white is supposed to be open and pure—can I make you feel enclosed and negative sometimes?

While working on *Daydreamers* I kept noticing that people were not looking at the children, and I tried to get readers to see the children's faces, to look into a very intimate book. Now because I'm concerned about what's happening with Black teenagers, and I want them to understand that everything they come from comes from their ancestors, I started working on a picture book. I came up with the themes and the ideas and I started doing the pictures. When I've finished all the pictures I'm going to give them to a writer to write the text. Like *Daydreamers*, the book will be intimate and will encourage real *looking* at the images in it.

The end papers and the title page of the new book will show the theme of a connection between Black people who have gone through a very painful situation but who had to work together to transcend it. That's why we're still here, that's why we're not killed off, and that's why we are going to continue to be here. The last picture is of all that energy in young Black males. This energy should be used in the best way but is often channeled into other things.

In this teenage picture book there is a special focus on the importance of books. You can find out about your past in reading, and it can help you deal with the present

Teenage Picture Book. Copyright © by Tom Feelings.

and the future. Deal with the slavery of the past by reading. Read for excitement. Your hopes and dreams will give you the ability to fly, help make choices about where you go with your life. In short, I want to see what Africa means to them, and what it means to all young people.

The following statement by Ayi Kwei Armah from *Two Thousand Seasons* talks about the responsibility of artists of color to the community they come from. When I read this statement, I substitute "artist" for the word "*fundi*."

Illustration by Tom Feelings. Copyright © by Tom Feelings.

The teachers told us quietly that the way of experts had become a tricky way. They told us it would always be fatal to our arts to misuse the skills we had learned. The skills themselves were mere light shells, needing to be filled out with substance coming from our souls. They warned us never to turn these skills to the service of things separate from the way. This would be the most difficult thing, for we would learn, they told us, that no *fundi* could work effectively when torn away from power, and yet power in these times lived far, immeasurably far from the way. This distance from the seats of power to the way, this distance now separating our way from power usurped against our people and our way, this distance would be the measure of the *fundi's* pain. They told us there was no light sweeter than that of the *fundi* in the bosom of his people if his people knew their way. But the life of a *fundi* whose people had lost their way is pain. All the excellence of such a *fundi's* craft is turned to trash. His skills are useless in the face of his people's destruction, and it is as easy as slipping on a riverstone to see his craftsmanship actually turned like a weapon against his people.

. . . Our way, the way, is not a random path. Our way begins from coherent understanding. It is a way that aims at preserving knowledge of who we are, knowledge of the best way we have found to relate each to each, each to all, ourselves to other peoples, all to our surroundings. If our individual's lives have a worthwhile aim, that aim should be a purpose inseparable from the way.

... Our way is reciprocity. The way is wholeness.[5]

I hope young artists listen to that. If you feel that you want to enter the mainstream in the book world, and by that I mean you feel that you have to illustrate white books and themes other than what you come out of, listen to what Ayi Kwei Armah is really saying. There are millions of your stories, yet untold. It is a way of exposing *your* people to their own self-worth and their humanity. It is the way of wholeness.

Notes:

1. Wilson, "I Don't Want to Hire Nobody Just 'Cause They're Black."
2. Ibid.
3. Ibid.
4. Hansberry, *To Be Young, Gifted and Black*.
5. Armah, *Two Thousand Seasons*, in *Living by the Word*, [10].

Works Cited:

Armah, Ayi Kwei, from *Two Thousand Seasons*. Chicago: Third World Press, 1979. Quoted in *Living By the Word: Selected Writings, 1973-1988*. By Alice Walker. San Diego: Harcourt Brace Jovanovich, 1988.

Caines, Jeannette. *Just Us Women*. Illustrated by Pat Cummings. New York: Harper & Row, 1982.

Carlstrom, Nancy White. *Wild , Wild Sunflower Child Anna*. Illustrated by Jerry Pinkney. New York: Macmillan, 1987.

Clifton, Lucille. *Everett Anderson's Nine Month Long*. New York: Holt, Rinehart & Winston, 1978.

Feelings, Tom. *Black Pilgrimage*. New York: Lothrop, Lee & Shepard, 1972.

Flournoy, Valerie. *The Best Time of Day*. Illustrated by George Ford. New York: Random House, 1978.

Greenberg, Polly. *Oh Lord, I Wish I Was a Buzzard*. Illustrated by Aliki. New York: Macmillan, 1968.

Greenfield, Eloise. *Daydreamers*. Illustrated by Tom Feelings. New York: Dial, 1981.

———.*Grandmama's Joy*. Illustrated by Carole Byard. New York: Collins, 1980.

———.*Paul Robeson*. Illustrated by George Ford. New York: Thomas Y. Crowell, 1975.

Grifalconi, Ann. *Osa's Pride*. Boston: Little, Brown, 1990.

Hansberry, Lorraine. *To Be Young, Gifted and Black*. New York: WNET-TV, 1972. Distributed by Indiana Univ. Film.

Isadora, Rachel. *Ben's Trumpet*. New York: Greenwillow, 1979.

Johnson, Angela. *Do Like Kyla*. Illustrated by James E. Ransome. New York: Orchard, 1990.

Johnson, James Weldon, and J. Rosamond Johnson. *Lift Every Voice and Sing: Words and Music*. Illustrated by Mozelle Thompson. New York: Hawthorn, 1970.

Keats, Ezra Jack. *The Snowy Day*. New York: Viking, 1962.

Lawrence, Jacob. *Harriet and the Promised Land*. New York: Windmill, 1968.

Shelby, Anne. *We Keep a Store*. Illustrated by John Ward. New York: Orchard, 1990.

Stanley, Diane, and Peter Vennema. *Shaka: King of the Zulus*. Illustrated by Diane Stanley. New York: Morrow, 1988.

Stock, Catherine. *Secret Valentine*. New York: Bradbury, 1991.

Williams, Karen Lynn. *Galimoto*. Illustrated by Catherine Stock. New York: Lothrop, 1990.

Williamson, Mel. *Walk On*. Illustrated by George Ford. New York: Third Press, 1972.

Wilson, August. "I Don't Want to Hire Nobody Just 'Cause They're Black." *New York Times*, Wednesday, 26 Sept. 1990, section A.

Yarbrough, Camille. *Cornrows*. Illustrated by Carole Byard. New York: Coward, McCann & Geoghegan, 1979.

Yezback, Steven A. *Pumpkinseeds*. Illustrated by Mozelle Thompson. New York: Macmillan, 1969.

A Selected Listing of Books by Tom Feelings:

Black Child. Written by Joyce Carol Thomas. Illustrated by Tom Feelings. New York: Zamani Productions, 1981.

Black Folktales. Written by Julius Lester. Illustrated by Tom Feelings. New York: Grove-Weidenfeld, 1970.

Black Pilgrimage. Written and illustrated by Tom Feelings. New York: Lothrop, Lee & Shepard, 1972.

Bola and the Oba's Drummers. Written by Letta Schatz. Illustrated by Tom Feelings. New York: McGraw-Hill, 1967.

The Congo, River of Mystery. Written by Robin McKown. Illustrated by Tom Feelings. New York: McGraw-Hill, 1968.

Daydreamers. Written by Eloise Greenfield. Illustrated by Tom Feelings. New York: Dial, 1981.

From Slave to Abolitionist: The Life of William Wells Brown. Written by Lucille Schulberg Warner. Illustrated by Tom Feelings. New York: Dial, 1976.

Jambo Means Hello. Written by Muriel Feelings. Illustrated by Tom Feelings. New York: Dial, 1974.

Moja Means One. Written by Muriel Feelings. Illustrated by Tom Feelings. New York: Dial, 1971.

A Quiet Place. Written by Rose Blue. Illustrated by Tom Feelings. New York: Franklin Watts, 1969.

Something on My Mind. Written by Nikki Grimes. Illustrated by Tom Feelings. New York: Dial, 1978.

Song of the Empty Bottles. Written by Osmond Molarsky. Illustrated by Tom Feelings. New York: H. Z. Walck, 1968.

Tales of Temba. Written by Kathleen Arnott. Illustrated by Tom Feelings. New York: H. Z. Walck, 1969.

To Be a Slave. Written by Julius Lester. Illustrated by Tom Feelings. New York: Dial, 1968.

Tommy Traveler in the World of Black History. Written and illustrated by Tom Feelings. New York: Black Butterfly, 1991.

Tuesday Elephant. Written by Nancy Garfield. Illustrated by Tom Feelings. New York: Seabury, 1970.

When the Stones Were Soft. Written by Eleanor B. Heady. Illustrated by Tom Feelings. New York: Funk & Wagnalls, 1968.

Zamani Goes to Market. Written by Muriel Feelings. Illustrated by Tom Feelings. New York: Seabury, 1970.

Going Around the Block
George Ancona

I grew up in Coney Island. It was the beginning of my adventures. I actually got up enough nerve to go around the block and, in a sense, that is what I've been doing the rest of my life. I just keep exploring and discovering through people.

I'm definitely a product of the so-called "melting pot." Growing up in this country I experienced a lot of spice and diversity, which opened up many doors for me.

George Ancona, "itinerant photographer." Copyright © by George Ancona.

As a teenager I loved sketching and painting by the Coney Island creek. I would sit for hours doing wood cuts. I was a quiet boy, and only later in life did I begin to get a perspective of why I was that way. My father was Mexican, but he was in the U.S. illegally so we always kept a low profile. The immigration people finally caught up with him, and I remember him saying, "But my son is a Boy Scout." We stayed. I had the good fortune of attending Lincoln High School where Mr. Leon Friend, a graphic design teacher, opened the world up to his students. In many ways, I'm still doing what he taught us: I'm still exploring.

George Ancona has been illustrating children's books with his photography since 1970. The son of Mexican parents from the Yucatan, he grew up in New York City. He studied at the Academy of San Carlos in Mexico and received an Art Students League scholarship in New York. He has worked with layout advertising and production at Esquire and Seventeen magazines, in various advertising agencies, and has made his own films. He has published more than 60 works; awards for his children's books include Notable Children's Books (American Library Association), Notable Children's Trade Books in the Field of Social Studies (National Council for the Social Studies/Children's Book Council), Outstanding Science Trade Books for Children (NSTA/ Children's Book Council), and the New York Times Best Books for Children. He currently lives with his family in Santa Fe, New Mexico.

After I graduated from high school, I went to Mexico and I thought, "I'm finally coming together with my people, this is where I belong, right?" My relatives listened to my Spanish, and they looked at my shoes and said, "Nah, you are a Gringo." So, I went back to New York.

After working for several years as an art director, I decided that it was more fun being a photographer, so I became one. I am an itinerant photographer — that means I'll pack up my things and head off to wherever I have to take pictures. As a free-lancer, it has sometimes been a little difficult to provide for my family all these years. But it has worked and I think my children are proud of what I am and the life that we've been able to live — which is one of exploration.

Discovering the world of books was a revelation, because I could work with what was inside of me. I could explore my own feelings, my own curiosities. I didn't have to wait for a purchase order or a client to say, "George, I'd like you to take this picture." It was a freedom, a discovery, and a search: the right to search for myself and what I wanted to say with my life and what I wanted to do.

I did my first book, *Faces*, with Barbara Brenner. It includes pictures of my children and my parents, along with many others. It's about the multiplicity of life and people around me.

One of the reasons I like being a free-lancer is that I can get my kids involved in what I do. The only trouble is, I keep asking them, "Doesn't anybody want to be a doctor or a lawyer?" They say, "No, Dad, we want to be free-lancers like you." One day my oldest son was pasting some papers down in architecture class and his schoolmate asked, "Where did you learn how to do that?" And Tom said, "I don't know." He thought a minute, and then added, "I guess I learned it from my father." We learn many, many things, not by going to school but just by observing, experiencing, and sharing time with an adult.

I love the quality of playing with kids with books; it becomes a game. Most importantly, it gives you a chance to be with children and hold them in your lap. I still love going to schools and sitting in kindergartens or older grades and just being with the children, because I get a sense of what they're responding to. When I see yawns, I know, "This is not very good, gotta get rid of it!"

From Dancing Is. Copyright © 1981 by George Ancona. Reprinted by permission of Penguin USA.

Dancing Is

If you grew up Hispanic in New York, you had to go dancing. Every Saturday and Sunday, you spent the afternoon dancing. When I was a little boy, my father taught me to dance. He would come home from work and put on a record. The music was from Mexico, the country where he grew up. He showed me how the cowboys there would dance the heel-stomping *zapateado*. I would imagine their boots raising the dust on a platform set outside the bunkhouse while guitars played and the men sang. Today it is my turn to dance around the living room with my children. When I dance I share my feelings with others. With *Dancing Is* I hope to share my feelings in the same way.

At times making this book was incredibly frustrating. I'd go to a party. There'd be music, there'd be lights, I'd shoot lots of pictures. Then I'd go into the darkroom and make a print, and it would be of someone frozen in space. So I decided to start manipulating the images, silhouetting them, making them move up and down on the page. To try on a two-dimensional level to capture that fourth dimension.

I explored the diversity of people's feelings and emotions in dancing. Dancing is moving to music. To dance, just listen to the music. The rhythm will tell you how to move. I could never understand going to a party and hearing someone say, "No, I don't like to dance" or "I don't want to dance." Of course you know how to dance. You've got to dance. (This is a battle I have with drawing and with painting—"No,

For this picture I got in touch with Louie Hopsi of the Thunderbird Society, who is a Hopi hoop dancer, and I said, "Louie, can you get me some dancers?" He said, "Sure." So early one Sunday morning he showed up with two truckloads of dancers. I was living in a little suburban area in New York. I found one small patch between the split level houses that had no clotheslines or TV aerials and the drums began. From Dancing Is by George Ancona. Copyright © 1981 by George Ancona. Reprinted by permission of Penguin USA.

I can't draw." What do you mean you can't draw? Of course you can draw. Everybody can draw.) Judging is so inhibiting. When you dance nobody will look at you or grade you. You just dance for yourself.

All over the world, people have their own dances. When they move away, they teach their children to dance the dances of the old country. By dancing, people remember the lands they came from, and their identity, and their cultures. Dancing provides continuity. I have been talking to some of the Pueblo people about this. Their young people are leaving the reservations and not coming back. These people are concerned about continuity. They've been in one place for 2,000 years, and this change is threatening to their way of life. And, as well as providing continuity, dances can change. For example, clogging became tap dancing.

Most people dance because it is fun. You can imagine the hard work and the dedication this book demanded of me: going to a party every Friday, Saturday, and Sunday—for a year! I truly hated to see this project end. It was one way I explored the joy and diversity and continuity of people. As I said, I'm still going around the block to see who else lives nearby.

The Indian classical dance tells stories about a frog jumping into a lake and coming out as the beautiful princess Mandodari. From Dancing Is by George Ancona. Copyright © 1981 by George Ancona. Reprinted by permission of Penguin USA.

Dancing in the Dominican Republic. From Dancing Is by George Ancona. Copyright © 1981 by George Ancona. Reprinted by permission of Penguin USA.

Selected Bibliography of Books by George Ancona:

The American Family Farm. Written by Joan Anderson. Photographs by George Ancona. San Diego: Harcourt Brace Jovanovich, 1989.

And What Do You Do? Written and photographed by George Ancona. New York: Dutton, 1976.

Aquarium. Written and photographed by George Ancona. New York: Clarion, 1990.

Artists of Handcrafted Furniture at Work. Written by Maxine B. Rosenberg. Photographs by George Ancona. New York: Lothrop, 1988.

Balance It! Written by Howard E. Smith, Jr. Photographs by George Ancona. New York: Four Winds Press, 1982.

Bananas: From Manolo to Margie. Written and photographed by George Ancona. New York: Clarion, 1982.

Being a Twin, Having a Twin. Written by Maxine B. Rosenberg. Photographs by George Ancona. New York: Lothrop, 1985.

Being Adopted. Written by Maxine B. Rosenberg. Photographs by George Ancona. New York: Lothrop, 1984.

Bodies. Written by Barbara Brenner. Photographs by George Ancona. New York: Dutton, 1973.

Christmas on the Prairie. Written by Joan Anderson. Photographs by George Ancona. New York: Clarion, 1985.

Christopher Columbus, From Vision to Voyage. Written by Joan Anderson. Photographs by George Ancona. New York: Dial, 1991.

City! New York. Written by Shirley Climo. Photographs by George Ancona. New York: Macmillan, 1990.

City! San Francisco. Written by Shirley Climo. Photographs by George Ancona. New York: Macmillan, 1990.

City! Washington, D.C. Written by Shirley Climo. Photographs by George Ancona. New York: Macmillan, 1991.

Dancing Is. Written and illustrated by George Ancona. New York: Dutton, 1981.

Dolphins at Grassy Key. Written by Marcia Seligson. Photographs by George Ancona. New York: Macmillan, 1989.

Faces. Written by Barbara Brenner. Photographs by George Ancona. New York: Dutton, 1970.

Finding a Way: Living with Exceptional Brothers and Sisters. Written by Maxine B. Rosenberg. Photographs by George Ancona. New York: Lothrop, 1988.

Finding Your First Job. Written by Sue Alexander. Photographs by George Ancona. New York: Dutton, 1980.

The First Thanksgiving Feast. Written by Joan Anderson. Photographs by George Ancona. New York: Clarion, 1984.

Freighters: Cargo Ships and People Who Work Them. Written and photographed by George Ancona. New York: Crowell, 1985.

From Map to Museum: Uncovering Mysteries of the Past. Written by Joan Anderson. Photographs by George Ancona. New York: Morrow, 1988.

The Glorious Fourth at Prairietown. Written by Joan Anderson. Photographs by George Ancona. New York: Morrow, 1986.

Grandpa Had a Windmill, Grandma Had a Churn. Written by Louise A. Jackson. Photographs by George Ancona. New York: Parents' Magazine Press, 1977.

Growing Older. Written and photographed by George Ancona. New York: Dutton, 1978.

Handtalk. Written by Remy Charlip, Mary B. Miller and George Ancona. Photographs by George Ancona. New York: Parents' Magazine Press, 1974.

Handtalk Birthday. Written by Remy Charlip, Mary B. Miller and George Ancona. Photographs by George Ancona. New York: Four Winds, 1987.

Handtalk School. Written by Mary Beth Miller and George Ancona. Photographs by George Ancona. New York: Four Winds, 1991.

Handtalk Zoo. Written by Mary B. Miller and George Ancona. Photographs by George Ancona. New York: Four Winds, 1989.

Harry's Helicopter. Written by Joan Anderson. Photographs by George Ancona. New York: Morrow, 1990.

Helping Out. Written and photographed by George Ancona. New York: Clarion, 1985.

I Feel. Written and photographed by George Ancona. New York: Dutton, 1977.

It's a Baby! Written and photographed by George Ancona. New York: Dutton, 1979.

Jackpot of the Beagle Brigade. Written by Sam and Beryl Epstein. Photographs by George Ancona. New York: Macmillan, 1987.

Joshua's Westward Journal. Written by Joan Anderson. Photographs by George Ancona. New York: Morrow, 1987.

Living in Two Worlds. Written by Maxine B. Rosenberg and Philip Spivey. Photographs by George Ancona. New York: Lothrop, 1986.

Making a New Home in America. Written by Maxine B. Rosenberg. Photographs by George Ancona. New York: Lothrop, 1986.

Mom Can't See Me. Written by Sally Alexander. Photographs by George Ancona. New York: Macmillan, 1990.

Monster Movers. Written and photographed by George Ancona. New York: Dutton, 1983.

Monsters on Wheels. Written and photographed by George Ancona. New York: Dutton, 1974.

My Feet Do. Written by Jean Holzenthaler. Photographs by George Ancona. New York: Dutton, 1979.

My Friend Leslie: The Story of a Handicapped Child. Written by Maxine B. Rosenberg. Photographs by George Ancona. New York: Lothrop, 1983.

My New Babysitter. Written by Christine Loomis. Photographs by George Ancona. New York: Morrow, 1991.

Over on the River. Written by Louise A. Jackson. Photographs by George Ancona. New York: Lothrop, 1980.

Pioneer Children of Appalachia. Written by Joan Anderson. Photographs by George Ancona. New York: Clarion, 1986.

Pioneer Settlers of New France. Written by Joan Anderson. Photographs by George Ancona. New York: Lodestar, 1990.

Riverkeeper. Written and photographed by George Ancona. New York: Macmillan, 1990.

Sheep Dog. Written and illustrated by George Ancona. New York: Lothrop, 1985.

Spanish Pioneers of the Southwest. Written by Joan Anderson. Photographs by George Ancona. New York: Lodestar, 1988.

Team Work. Written and photographed by George Ancona. New York: Crowell, 1983.

Turtle Watch. Written and photographed by George Ancona. New York: Macmillan, 1987.

A Williamsburg Household. Written by Joan Anderson. Photographs by George Ancona. New York: Clarion, 1988.

Publisher's Perspective

Phoebe Yeh
Scholastic Inc.

As the fifth largest publisher in the elementary and secondary school market, Scholastic's access to the young reading public is undeniable. In our magazine division we publish 26 school magazines with a readership of over 2.3 million students. We maintain a huge paperback distribution program through the Scholastic Book Clubs, the oldest and the largest of the school book clubs, and the Scholastic school book fairs, servicing children and educators in preschools, elementary schools, intermediate schools, and high schools.

We believe our starting point should be with child appeal and interest level; thus, the success of our Clifford books (Clifford the Big Red Dog, beloved canine who graces the pages of more than 22 million Clifford books in seven different languages), the Babysitters Club series, and for older readers, Scholastic's "clean" response to the horror genre, comes as no surprise.

Because our books are sent directly into classrooms through our book clubs, much of our publishing program is specially created to address the needs and interests of young readers, as well as what we feel children want to read, and what teachers are seeking for their students. In recent years, educators have become extremely enthusiastic about using trade books in the classroom. Often they are looking for literature with a science or social studies component to supplement textbooks or sometimes, even to supplant textbooks. Certainly, *Fallen Angels* provides a more provocative and compelling way to learn about the Vietnam War than a history textbook.

In the best of all possible worlds, we could successfully sell a multicultural piece of literature, fiction, or nonfiction, at any time in the year. In all honesty, particularly in the school market venue, this is still not a practical reality. Thus, *The Mud Pony*, a Pawnee tale for which we deliberately found a Native American illustrator, is sold in October and November, when most teachers seem to teach their units on

Phoebe Yeh is a picture book editor at Scholastic Inc. Prior to her current editorial position, she was the editor of Seesaw Book Club, a Scholastic paperback school book club. She attended Amherst College and after graduating spent a year in Taiwan teaching English. Ms. Yeh lives in New York City.

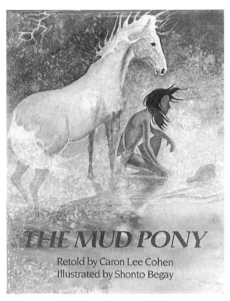

THE MUD PONY

Retold by Caron Lee Cohen
Illustrated by Shonto Begay

The Mud Pony. Copyright © 1988 Text by Caron Lee Cohen, Illus. by Shanto Begay. Reprinted with permission of Scholastic Inc.

Native Americans. *Rain Forest Secrets* is sold in the spring, just in time for Earth Day.

It will come as no surprise when I say that in January and February we're flooded with requests from teachers for books about Dr. Martin Luther King. Jr. and other African-American heroes, contemporary stories with African-American protagonists, and for books about Asian cultures and Asian-Americans who celebrate the lunar new year. Bookstores and libraries also commemorate the occasions with special window and book displays. People want to buy these books in January and February, but we have found interest to slacken during the rest of the year. While we do not believe that children should be exposed to titles like *Mufaro's Beautiful Daughters* and *Lion Dancer* in only two months of the year, our sales indicate to us that books with multicultural characters and themes sell far better when teachers and parents connect them with holidays and special events. It may seem limiting to sell *I Hate English* and *Angel Child, Dragon Child* only during the lunar new year or in time for Asian Pacific Heritage month, but our sales show that we are reaching far more children at these times than at other times of the year. Until the day arrives when children and adults buy books indiscriminately with regard to the holiday calendar, isn't it preferable for children to buy these books in January and February, rather than not at all? On the other hand, surely holidays and specially designated months are not the only times to expose children to cultural diversity.

Our biography publishing program serves two functions. First, biographies are immensely popular among middle-grade readers. They also provide a way to introduce children to contemporary African-American leaders in a format to which they are receptive. Most publishers have produced biographies about the lives of Harriet Tubman, George Washington Carver, and Dr. Martin Luther King, Jr. Of course, these titles also number among our backlist, but we purposefully work to introduce children to contemporary leaders. Thus, two recent additions to our hardcover list are biographies on the lives of Nelson Mandela and the Reverend Jesse Jackson.

On the flip side, just as adults are fascinated with the lives of film, music, and sports celebrities, children, too, are curious about their media idols. We recently responded to trends in teen popular culture by releasing a dual biography on

Lion Dancer. Copyright © Text 1990 by Kate Waters, Photographs 1990 by Martha Cooper. Reprinted with permission of Scholastic, Inc.

rappers M. C. Hammer and Vanilla Ice. In biographies such as this, we have found an effective way to reach reluctant readers.

About five years ago, when other publishers started their own paperback divisions, our response was to create a hardcover publishing program. Although it's not easy being the new kid on the block, it provides an impetus to be more innovative and to take more risks in acquisitions. Certainly, the Scholastic hardcover list reflects our commitment to seek out books we think children will find appealing and accessible, but it is also characterized by a willingness to explore "non-traditional" venues in format and design, and to acquire books we feel children need in a pluralistic society.

Mary Had a Little Lamb, photo-illustrated by Bruce McMillan, and *The Seven Chinese Brothers*, retold by Margaret Mahy and illustrated by Jean and Mou-sien Tseng, are two books which reflect Scholastic's attempt to bring old favorites into the twenty-first century. In *Mary Had a Little Lamb*, Bruce McMillan offers the traditional New England poem with a twist. Mary is an African-American child, sporting glasses, and has a lamb who follows her everywhere she goes.

First published in 1938, *The Five Chinese Brothers*, written by Claire Huchet Bishop and illustrated by Kurt Wiese, remained a popular book in the United States for many years. The folktale was one of my favorites from childhood, but I read a different version about five Liu brothers, who have super magical powers. The pictures in my book were more realistic than the yellow-faced caricatures in Mr. Wiese's artwork. Some 50 years after the original publication of *The Five Chinese Brothers*, Scholastic decided that it was time to bring the folktale back. We found versions with five, seven, and ten brothers. Our research also revealed a version that made reference to the Great Wall and Emperor Chin Shih Huang. We were committed to finding a Chinese writer for our book, but the several Chinese-American writers we contacted were not interested in retelling the folktale. Margaret Mahy *was* interested, but wondered if she could do justice to the tale with her "Western" literary background. Ms. Mahy's witty storytelling in *The Seven Chinese Brothers* shows sensitivity and proves that you don't have to be born into a culture to do justice to its folklore.

With our search for a writer completed, we then had to decide on an illustrator. Again, we were committed to finding a Chinese illustrator. The Tsengs proved an ideal choice. They spent months carefully researching the hairstyles, clothing, even footwear and arms carried by warriors of the period. They capture the richness and color of the first imperial court with authenticity. In an interesting note about authenticity: I asked the Tsengs how they felt about non-Asians illustrating Asian folktales and Mou-sien's response bears some consideration. In paraphrase, he said, "While an illustrator with Western heritage or training may not always present the most accurate interpretation of an Asian folktale, his perspective is still unique and something I couldn't have thought of. I'm interested in how his interpretation differs from mine."

Arroz con Leche and *The Black Snowman* are books by author/illustrators who came to us with stories from their own personal experience after previously publishing very different types of work with Scholastic. Lulu Delacre, editor and illustrator of *Arroz con Leche*, is the creator of a series about an elephant and his best friend, *Nathan and Nicholas Alexander*. After Lulu had her first child, she wanted to share the nursery rhymes and songs from her Puerto Rican childhood with her daughter, but couldn't find any children's books with this kind of information. *Arroz con Leche*, a bilingual collection of Spanish songs, rhymes, and games from Latin America, is the result. The book also offers descriptions of traditions associated with each song, truly a legacy to Lulu's children and an important contribution to cultural awareness. The tremendous response to the first title guaranteed a follow-up, *Las Navidades*, a similar format with a Christmas theme. Who says there isn't a market for Latino books?

Phil Mendez came to Scholastic through our Kissyfur license, based on the animated cartoon series. While working on the Kissyfur books, Phil gave us a manuscript titled *The Black Snowman*, a story loosely based on his own experience of growing up Black in America. In an urban contemporary Christmas story, a dis-

illusioned African-American boy learns about his heritage when a slushy black snowman presents him with a magical kente cloth. African-American artist Carole Byard's compelling artwork illustrates this story about self-worth and courage.

At Scholastic, we believe that "multicultural" extends beyond ethnic groups in America. We were proud to publish the first American-Russian children's book in the United States, *Here Comes the Cat!*, designed by American Frank Asch and painted by Russian Vladimir Vagin. In cartoon speech bubbles, an

Arroz con Leche. Copyright © 1989 by Lulu Delacre. Reprinted by permission of Scholastic, Inc.

alarmed mouse warns the other mice about an approaching cat, who, in fact, is actually bringing a huge cheese wheel to the mice. When *Rehema's Journey*, written and illustrated in photos by Barbara Margolies, was acquired, media attention was focused on the famine in Ethiopia. Since there are so few books about African children available to American children, we hoped in *Rehema's Journey* to show a happy, healthy Tanzanian child experiencing a first trip away from home, and dispel some of the popular misconceptions American children may have about their counterparts in Africa (at least in Tanzania).

In *The Best Teacher in the World*, by Bernice Chardiet and Grace Maccarone, I made a conscious decision to make the teacher, Ms. Darcy, African-American. It's not enough to present a "racial mix" of students in a classroom setting. By making Ms. Darcy African-American, I wanted to send a message to children about an African-American role model of authority. We were not all in agreement over this decision, and now in retrospect I wonder, if I hadn't made a point of making this suggestion, would it have occurred to anyone else?

What Mary Jo Shared, by Janice May Udry, is a story about a shy African-American girl who worries about having something new for "show and tell." Finally she comes up with the perfect idea: she brings her father, who is a high school teacher, and the class is fascinated by his stories about his mischievous childhood. When we realized how dated the artwork was in our 1966 version, we asked the original publisher for permission to create new artwork for the story, rather than put the book out of print.

Fallen Angels. Copyright © 1988 by Walter Dean Myers. Reprinted with permission of Scholastic, Inc.

Our young adult novels reflect our willingness to take risks in our publishing program, to explore new, sometimes controversial, sometimes uncommon, subjects. *How Many Spots Does a Leopard Have?* is a collection of African-American *and* Jewish folktales by Julius Lester. Another young adult novel, *Fallen Angels* by Walter Dean Myers, is a coming of age Vietnam story that contains language and subject matter that may be considered controversial, especially in the school market venue. *Wolf by the Ears*, by Ann Rinaldi, offers another example of our willingness to take risks. This book was rejected by another publishing house before it came to Scholastic because of the potentially "sensitive" nature of the storyline: a diary format tells of the biracial young woman rumored to be the daughter of Thomas Jefferson.

I'm happy to say that all of the above books reflect the work of many different editors at Scholastic, not just the Asian-American on board. While we realize that there is still a long way to go, we've made a promising start. I encourage writers and artists of color to send in manuscripts and art samples. Make a point of telling us who you are. Take advantage of the "multicultural" climate. May it prevail.

Works Cited:

Bishop, Claire Huchet. *The Five Chinese Brothers*. Illustrated by Kurt Wiese. New York: Coward-McCann, 1938.

Chardiet, Bernice, and Grace Maccarone. *The Best Teacher in the World*. Illustrated by G. Brian Karas. New York: Scholastic/Hardcover, 1990.

Cohen, Caron Lee. *The Mud Pony: A Traditional Skidi Pawnee Tale*. Illustrated by Shonto Begay. New York: Scholastic/Hardcover, 1988.

Delacre, Lulu, editor and illustrator. *Arroz con Leche: Popular Songs and Rhymes from Latin America*. New York: Scholastic/Hardcover, 1989.

———. *Las Navidades: Popular Christmas Songs from Latin America*. Lyrics translated into English by Elena Paz. Music arranged by Ana-Maria Rosado. New York: Scholastic/Hardcover, 1990.

———. *Nathan and Nicholas Alexander*. New York: Scholastic, 1986.

Denenberg, Barry. *Nelson Mandela: No Easy Walk to Freedom*. New York: Scholastic/Hardcover, 1991.

Dorros, Arthur. *Rain Forest Secrets*. New York: Scholastic/Hardcover, 1990.

Hale, Sarah Josepha. *Mary Had a Little Lamb*. Photo-illustrated by Bruce McMillan. New York: Scholastic/Hardcover, 1990.

Krulik, Nancy E. *M. C. Hammer and Vanilla Ice: The Hip-hop Never Stops!* New York: Scholastic, 1991, pbk.

Lester, Julius. *How Many Spots Does a Leopard Have? . . . And Other Tales*. Illustrated by David Shannon. New York: Scholastic/Hardcover, 1989.

Levine, Ellen. *I Hate English!* Illustrated by Steven Björkman. New York: Scholastic/Hardcover, 1989.

Mahy, Margaret, *The Seven Chinese Brothers*. Illustrated by Jean and Mou-sien Tseng. New York: Scholastic/Hardcover, 1990.

Margolies, Barbara A. *Rehema's Journey: A Visit to Tanzania*. New York: Scholastic, 1990.

McKissack, Patricia C. *Jesse Jackson: A Biography*. New York: Scholastic/Hardcover, 1989.

Mendez, Phil. *The Black Snowman*. Illustrated by Carole Byard. New York: Scholastic/Hardcover, 1989.

Myers, Walter Dean. *Fallen Angels*. New York: Scholastic/Hardcover, 1988.

Rinaldi, Ann. *Wolf by the Ears*. New York: Scholastic/Hardcover, 1991.

Steptoe, John. *Mufaro's Beautiful Daughters: An African Tale*. New York: Lothrop, Lee & Shepard, 1987.

Surat, Michele Maria. *Angel Child, Dragon Child*. Illustrated by Vo-Dinh Mai. Milwaukee, WI: Raintree, 1983. New York: Scholastic, 1989, pbk.

Udry, Janice May. *What Mary Jo Shared*. Illustrated by Elizabeth Sayles. New York: Scholastic, 1991, pbk.

Vagin, Vladimir, and Frank Asch. *Here Comes the Cat!* (U.S. edition) New York: Scholastic/Hardcover, 1989.

Waters, Kate, and Madeline Slovenz-Low. *Lion Dancer: Ernie Wan's Chinese New Year*. Photographs by Martha Cooper. New York: Scholastic/Hardcover, 1990

A Selected List of Scholastic Books Edited by Phoebe Yeh:

Editor

Chardiet, Bernice and Grace Maccarone. *The Best Teacher in the World*. Illustrated by G. Brian Karas. New York: Scholastic/Hardcover, 1990.

———. *Brenda's Private Swing*. Illustrated by G. Brian Karas. New York: Scholastic, 1991, pbk.

———. *Martin and the Teacher's Pets*. Illustrated by G. Brian Karas. New York: Scholastic, 1991, pbk.

———. *Martin and the Tooth Fairy*. Illustrated by G. Brian Karas. New York: Scholastic/Hardcover, 1991.

———. *Merry Christmas, What's Your Name*. Illustrated by G. Brian Karas. New York: Scholastic/Hardcover, 1990.

Dorros, Arthur. *Animal Tracks*. New York: Scholastic/Hardcover, 1991.

———. *Me and My Shadow*. New York: Scholastic/Hardcover, 1990.

———. *Rain Forest Secrets*. New York: Scholastic/Hardcover, 1990.

Kowitt, Holly. *The Fenderbenders Get Lost in America*. New York: Scholastic, 1991, pbk.

Maestro, Betsy. *A Sea Full of Sharks*. Illustrated by Giulio Maestro. New York: Scholastic/Hardcover, 1990.

———. *Snow Day*. Illustrated by Giulio Maestro. New York: Scholastic/Hardcover, 1989.

Mahy, Margaret. *The Seven Chinese Brothers*. Illustrated by Jean and Mou-sien Tseng. New York: Scholastic/Hardcover, 1990.

Margolies, Barbara A. *Rehema's Journey: A Visit in Tanzania*. With photos by the author. New York: Scholastic/Hardcover, 1990.

Slepian, Jan and Ann Seidler. *The Hungry Thing Returns*. New York: Scholastic/Hardcover, 1990.

Co-editor

Cole, Joanna. *The Magic School Bus at the Waterworks*. Illustrated by Bruce Degen. New York: Scholastic/Hardcover, 1986.

———. *The Magic School Bus Inside the Earth*. Illustrated by Bruce Degen. New York: Scholastic/Hardcover, 1987.

———. *The Magic School Bus Inside the Human Body*. Illustrated by Bruce Degen. New York: Scholastic/Hardcover, 1989.

———. *The Magic School Bus Lost in the Solar System*. Illustrated by Bruce Degen. New York: Scholastic/Hardcover, 1990.

Wade Hudson
Just Us Books

I grew up in a small, very segregated town in Louisiana. Anyone who knows about segregation, oppression, and racism, knows these evil institutions feed on miseducation and the lack of education. So, the textbooks in our school and the books in our library had virtually nothing about Black people. We were told Black people had done hardly anything important. The books we could read that mentioned Black people at all were there to prove that. We were told this was their world, and we, Black people, were just the white man's burden.

James Baldwin, Ralph Ellison, W.E.B. Dubois, and Zora Neale Hurston did not exist for me. But I felt, even at nine and ten years of age, that Black people had a story to tell. We have a history and a past. Many times my grandfather had captivated me with his intriguing stories of our ancestors. My mother would hold court for an hour talking about older relatives and the interesting things they had done. I knew other Black people had important things to say, too. But why weren't books written by and about Black people?

At the age of ten, I decided I was going to write—and I did. I wrote my first book in pencil; I stapled the pages together and put the title on the front page in big, bold, crooked letters. I was smart. I didn't do just one copy. I understood profit and gain even at that age. I did three copies and sold two of them.

I didn't understand what publishing was all about. I just thought that there should be something written about Black people for others to read. That belief I held as a child is the reason my wife and I formed Just Us Books three years ago. We wanted to present a rich and fertile African-American heritage to young readers that was not available at that time. Once we sat down and started to make plans for our books, we found out that publishing is a business—a big business with many aspects to it. Publishers must consider marketing, production, manufacturing, sales, promotion, distribution, and of course, editing and design.

Wade Hudson, a former public relations specialist, is a playwright, poet and freelance writer. He attended Southern University in Louisiana and the Television and Film School at WNET - Channel 13 in New York City. Wade Hudson and Cheryl Willis Hudson founded Just Us Books in 1987.

All of these components are important to the success of a book. If you have a book (and it can be the kind of book that we all desire) and nobody knows about the book, it is not going to sell. It is not going to be available to the public. I think it is important that we consider the importance of people of color being involved in all of the vitally important aspects of publishing, including the marketing, the sale, and the promotion. Publishing is more than just finding a good book to produce.

I have seen a lot of good books, but many children, particularly those in the African-American community, are not aware of these books. This has become clear to us as we work at book fairs. Parents who come to these book fairs often are seeing much of the available authentic multicultural literature for the first time. Many of these books were published ten to fifteen years ago. Prior to the book fair, the parents and children didn't know that these books existed. Book stores in their communities do not carry these books. These stores say they don't see a viable market for the books. If publishers had seriously considered promotions and sales in the framework of multicultural publishing, this would not be the case.

I would like to see Random House, Macmillan, and other major publishing houses publish more books that reflect the mosaic that is America. I would also like to see African-Americans and other ethnic people institute and set up their own publishing houses to offer alternatives. There is no reason why we should not be doing that ourselves, as well as holding the major publishing houses accountable for what they should be doing.

We cannot look for one single answer. We must look at the total picture of what is happening, and that total picture includes taking our own destiny in our own hands and instituting those kinds of businesses that will support and sustain us. There are Jewish presses and Catholic presses; why shouldn't there be African-American presses or Native American presses? Small presses are alternatives to the major publishing houses.

Just Us Books was formed about three years ago and it has been a struggle ever since. We've learned as we have gone along. We have published seven books since starting the company, and we now have over 350,000 books in print; a figure that is amazing for a small publishing house. Our success is directly linked to our ability to reach a market that the major publishing houses have not found. They may never reach those markets (and again, this touches on the other components of the publishing process such as marketing and promotion) because they don't *know* my community. I know more about the buying habits of my community than anybody else, because I live in that community. I know the institutions, clubs, and organizations in that community, and I know how to tap into them. If people of color are employed in marketing, sales positions, and promotions, as well as editorial positions, their knowledge and place in the community will prove invaluable. It is the only way that we can make a total difference in terms of producing quality books and getting them into the hands of the children.

As I mentioned above, Just Us Books has published over 350,000 books in the past three years, and because of that success, we are getting calls from major publishing houses looking to us to suggest marketing strategies, ideas, and concepts, because they see that financial profit is linked to that knowledge they are lacking. Economics is the bottom-line and there is nothing wrong with it; we want to sell our books too! If we can't sell our books, then we will not be in business long. As a business—one that can sustain itself and continue to grow and offer opportunities to others in our own community—it also generates money that will go into our community so we can continue to build other institutions as well.

Editing, design, and content are crucial factors in the publishing business, but not the only ones. We must evaluate the total process, and recognize the importance and roles of all the aspects involved.

Cheryl Hudson
Just Us Books

In thinking and planning for a conference on multicultural literature for children, I had some immediate responses. I was very excited about the possibilities and after speaking with the conference planners, I was even more intrigued, especially by the title: "The Multicolored Mirror: Cultural Substance in Literature for Children and Young Adults." Immediately, I began to free-associate: Multi/Many, Color/Mirror, Mirror/Reflection, Reflection/Images, Images/Brilliance, Color/Rainbow, Rainbow/Spectrum, Color/Culture, Culture/Color, and so on. But, after free-associating for a few moments, a childhood memory came back to haunt me. It came back in the form of these words: "Mirror, mirror on the wall, who's the fairest of them all?" We all know the response. The mirror said that Snow White was the fairest. Fair implying fragile, feminine, innocent, pale, ingenue, light, lovely. It wasn't until my early adulthood that I openly questioned the movie or the fairy tale, or the assumptions. I realized all that stuff about fairness was just propaganda. I can submit to you today, some 20 years later, that Snow White wasn't reflected in a multicolored mirror. Neither she nor the wicked witch nor the dwarfs (i.e., little people) knew anything about affirmative action, or equity, or demographics, or publishing for that matter. The image of Snow White and her story remains with me. Hollywood knew what it was doing. But, as a parent and a publishing professional, I have a responsibility to provide perspective.

Publishers have tremendous power. Tremendous power to present ideas and images. They have the power to question assumptions so that they are not guilty of producing propaganda or pablum. It's a big responsibility and it's a responsibility that Just Us Books is trying to address. Multicultural literature is grounded in the values of people of color. At Just Us Books, it means commitment to an African-American centered perspective. This perspective is important for reasons of policy and practice.

Just Us Books creates and publishes books for children that focus on the African-American experience. They are targeted to an African-American audience, but

Cheryl Willis Hudson is a graphic artist and book designer. She is a graduate of Oberlin College, and has designed books for Houghton Mifflin, Macmillan, Hayden, and Paperwing Press. Her stories and illustrations for children have appeared in Ebony Jr. and Wee Wisdom Magazine. Wade Hudson and Cheryl Willis Hudson founded Just Us Books in 1987.

they are accessible and valuable to all children. We believe that they are authentic, culturally specific yet global, and yes, universal.

Now, getting back to publishing policy and practice. In our perspective, we consider the following list of factors that we try to embody in the manuscripts and in the illustrations we select:

- A commitment to a value-centered publishing philosophy.

- Accountability and respect for our audience.

- Positive images that leave lasting impressions.

- Accurate, factual information that's also enjoyable to read.

- Cultural authenticity.

- Cultural specificity.

- Meaningful stories that reflect a range of African-American values and lifestyles.

- A perspective that is clear on the positive aspects of being a person of color on the planet Earth in the twenty-first century.

- Non-fiction that is relevant to issues in today's world.

- Material that is self-affirming.

- Presentation of strong, three-dimensional characters.

- Well-written information.

- Attractive graphics.

- Durability

- Affordability.

- Images that our children can value and want to look at more than once.

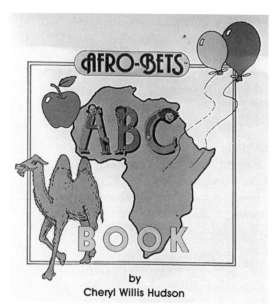

by
Cheryl Willis Hudson

Afro-Bets ABC Book. Copyright © 1987 by Cheryl Willis Hudson. Reprinted by permission of Just Us Books.

In conclusion, what we want is a nice, little package that functions as a book ought. A vehicle which opens the windows of knowledge, information, and self-discovery.

In our publishing strategy, we deliberately started out with an alphabet book—a concept book for infants and toddlers.[1] "A" is for apple, but it is also for alligator and Africa. "B" is for balloon and baseball, but it is also for brown baby. "C" is for car, camel, and corn rows. In *Afro-Bets First Book of Black Heroes from A to Z*, we talk about our heroes. Not just one at a time, but over 49 of them: Paul Robeson, Frederick Douglass, Edmonia Lewis, as well as Mary McLeod Bethune and Martin Luther King, Jr. In the *Afro-Bets First Book about Africa* we're not afraid to say Africa is the beginning. In *Bright Eyes, Brown Skin*, we refer to an African-American's nose as "perfect." Not flat, not broad, not pug, but perfect for an African-American face.

Afro-Bets Books of Black Heroes from A to Z. Copyright © 1988 by Just Us Books, a division of Just Us Productions, Inc. Reprinted by permission of Just Us Books.

Our publishing perspective makes no apologies. We are valuable because we are. The larger mainstream publishing companies have the same responsibilities that we do. Yes, other publishers can publish African-American writers and illustrators, and they should. But in order to do this with perspective and authenticity, their publishing plan must be fair, and I have a different definition of fair and affirmative. There must be positive and aggressive action in hiring, training, and retaining people of color as editors, artists, art directors, managers.

Some publishers have strange ideas about policy and practice, but that is changing. Conferences like The Multicolored Mirror facilitate dialogue, and honest and healthy reexamination of materials. This can be enlightening, and it can be a little bit scary, because we really have to examine our beliefs and our assumptions.

In the book *Megatrends 2000*, John Naisbitt and Patricia Aburdene write: "The more homogeneous our lifestyles become, the more steadfastly we shall cling to deeper values; religion, language, art, and literature. As our outer worlds become more similar, we will increasingly treasure the traditions that spring from within."[2]

At Just Us Books, we value and treasure our traditions. Now when I think about the quotation and the question "Mirror, mirror on the wall, who's the fairest of them all?" I'm not associating fairness or fair with whiteness, or paleness, or lack of color. I see fair as equitable, and I see, in this mirror, true colors, shining. True colors shining, true colors beautiful like a rainbow.

83

Bright eyes...

Bright Eyes, Brown Skin. Copyright © 1990 by Cheryl Willis Hudson and Bernette G. Ford. Illustrations, 1990 by George Ford. Reprinted by permission of Just Us Books.

Notes:

1. Hudson, *Afro-Bets ABC Book*.
2. Naisbitt, *Megatrends 2000*, 120.

Works Cited:

Ellis, Veronica Freeman. *Afro-Bets First Book about America*. Illustrated by George Ford. Orange, NJ: Just Us Books, 1989.

Hudson, Cheryl Willis. *Afro-Bets ABC Book*. Orange, NJ: Just Us Books, 1987.

Hudson, Cheryl Willis, and Bernette G. Ford. *Bright Eyes, Brown Skin*. Illustrated by George Ford. Orange, NJ: Just Us Books, 1990.

Hudson, Wade, and Valerie Wilson Wesley. *Afro-Bets Book of Black Heroes from A To Z: An Introduction to Important Black Achievers*. Orange, NJ: Just Us Books, 1988.

Naisbitt, John, and Patricia Aburdene. M*egatrends 2000: Ten New Directions for the 1990's*. New York: William Morrow, 1990.

Just Us Books Publications

Afro-Bets ABC Book by Cheryl Willis Hudson. Orange, NJ: Just Us Books, 1987.

Afro-Bets Activity and Enrichment Handbook. Orange, NJ: Just Us Books, 1990.

Afro-Bets Book of Black Heroes from A to Z by Wade Hudson and Valerie Wilson Wesley. Orange, NJ: Just Us Books, 1988.

Afro-Bets Coloring and Activity Book illustrated by Dwayne Ferguson. Orange, NJ: Just Us Books, 1990.

Afro-Bets First Book about Africa by Veronica Ellis Freeman. Illustrated by George Ford. Orange, NJ: Just Us Books, 1990.

Afro-Bets 1 2 3 Book by Cheryl Willis Hudson. Orange, NJ: Just Us Books, 1988.

Bright Eyes, Brown Skin by Cheryl Willis Hudson and Bernette G. Ford. Illustrated by George Ford. Orange, NJ: Just Us Books, 1990.

Publisher's Panel
Question and Answer

QUESTION: In your experience, do you think that the juvenile publishing industry is open to publishing books by writers and artists of color? Is there anything in particular that your company is doing to find and nurture authors and artists of color?

P. YEH: Some of the books that I showed you this afternoon are a direct response to what we want to be doing more of in our juvenile publishing. Every time we find a writer or artist of color we try very hard to publish this person, if possible. Often these people are first time artists, in the writing and illustrating sense. I think we can show our continuing commitment by immediately signing them up for another project. Recently we have encouraged writers to tell their own stories, in addition to, for example, those which might be their typical assignments as free-lance work. The discovery that Lulu Delacre, Phil Mendez, and others had very viable stories of their own that we wanted to get into the literature was new to us. I think we are trying hard. I took a quick look at the last 100 unsolicited manuscripts directed to my attention at Scholastic. As far as I know, two were written by people of color. That's not a lot. I think that we are going to try harder and harder in the upcoming years. Part of what we do in our school market, that is, in our book clubs, is find books published by other houses that we think kids need to be reading, and teachers need to be using in their classrooms. This is one way to compensate for a lack of these materials, at least until we can produce more original publishing.

W. HUDSON: I think some publishers are more receptive to authors and illustrators of color than others. But, in talking to a lot of editors, I hear, "We would like to have more African-American writers or artists, but they're not available. Where are they?" That is really a standard excuse for not finding them. They are out there. I think pressure is being brought to bear from a number of areas on publishers to be more sensitive to the mosaic that is America, and to produce books that are representative of what we are as a country. Scholastic is probably one of the better publishing companies in terms of publishing a variety of books, but other publishers are more difficult to convince. I think we have to continually make them aware of it and raise hell, so to speak, from all corners to let them know that we want books reflective of our society.

QUESTION: Something that you said, Phoebe, raises a question that I am frequently asked. It is, and Wade and Cheryl can answer this as well: "When you receive an unsolicited manuscript, do you always know the race or ethnic background of the author or artist, and does it matter?

P. YEH: It doesn't matter to me, but much depends on the cover letter. There are many editors at Scholastic, and I can't speak for them all, but it shouldn't matter. Unless portfolios come through the mail, editors do actually meet the illustrators, but most of our manuscripts come through the mail. Technically, you would not necessarily know the race of a book creator unless he or she gives hints in the letter. I encourage authors, if they are comfortable doing so, to indicate just who they are in their cover letters. It's very helpful to those who are committed to expanding their publishing program in this manner. Sometimes an editor can tell by the nature of the story, but not always.

We're just looking for the best stories out there, stories that we think kids in a pluralistic society need to be exposed to. Ultimately, we don't select books for our hardcover program along color lines. However, when we feel there is a need for a particular story to tell, Nelson Mandela's story for example, then we are committed to bringing such a book out. It is a two-way process.

C. HUDSON: I think the race of the book creator makes a difference, primarily in terms of who the writer is and sometimes the illustrator as well. Tom Feelings made this point in terms of style and approach to illustration. It's important that the artist know the direction of the book and is grounded in the culture being illustrated. Many things might be missed by someone who did not grow up and live in that culture. That's not to say that non-African-Americans cannot draw African-Americans, but in our publishing company it is our policy and practice to encourage African-American artists. There are very few African-American illustrators who are working. I've heard some art agents say that it doesn't matter. It does matter—there's a kind of color blindness that may automatically exclude certain kinds of people.

I worked in major publishing companies and was brought to task early in my career for bringing too many Black people into the building. I was working in a publishing company in Boston and at the same time working with a photography project at MIT where photographers were being trained in Roxbury. In the 1970s, a great many books were being illustrated with photography. So when I met these photographers at MIT, I said, "Come in and show us your portfolio." On a succession of days, several of the photographers came into the publishing office in response to my invitation. At that time, I was the only Black person working in the art department. I don't know what they thought was going to happen but one of the editors called me to task and said, "You have too many Black people coming in here." He was trying to be nice.

An all-white world or a kind of closed society, as publishing often is, can be intimidating. The industry has changed in some ways, but it has not changed a lot from the kind of perceptions that were mentioned in Nancy Larrick's study in 1965. If you went back to Boston, to the same publishing company I worked at, you would probably find that they have not hired another Black art director in that particular area since then, and that was 20 years ago. It is very important to have the knowledge of the cultural background for the authenticity of the art work. But it is also important to have people in positions to be able to recognize talent when they see it. Sometimes you may not recognize the talent in the manuscript because you are not tuned into it. It works in both directions.

Authentic Multicultural Literature for Children: An Author's Perspective

Elizabeth Fitzgerald Howard

> *. . . I love a lot of things, a whole lot of things*
> *Like*
> *my cousin comes to visit and you know he's from the South*
> *'Cause every word he says just kind of slides out of his mouth*
> *I like the way he whistles and I like the way he walks*
> *But honey, let me tell you that I LOVE the way he talks*
>> *I love the way my cousin talks*
>>> *and*
> *The day is hot and icky and the sun sticks to my skin*
> *Mr. Davis turns the hose on, everybody jumps right in*
> *The water stings my stomach and I feel so nice and cool*
> *Honey, let me tell you that I LOVE a flying pool*
>> *I love to feel a flying pool . . .* [1]

I wish I had written that; thank you, Eloise Greenfield! Honey, let me tell you that I just *love* Eloise Greenfield! She is one of the African-American authors currently writing authentic books portraying African-American experiences for all children.

What is authenticity? The dictionary lists synonyms for authentic: true, real, and genuine. These words fan out to become: verifiable, legitimate, solid, positive, concrete, honest, tangible, imaginable. We must seek the truth in the interpretation of African-American experience in specific children's books, but at the same time, we are seeking more. We must go a step further to add up those specific books and ask whether we are yet producing in the United States an authentic body of African-American literature for children. A body of literature meaning quantity, which includes all genres. There is a need for more poetry, for more biography, for

---

Elizabeth Fitzgerald Howard is a professor of Library Science at West Virginia University. She holds degrees from Radcliffe College and the University of Pittsburgh. She has worked as a teacher of children's literature and a children's librarian. Ms. Howard and her husband, Lawrence C. Howard, a professor of Public and International Affairs at the University of Pittsburgh, have three daughters and two grandchildren.

more fantasy. We also must aim for that authentic body of literature for children which can lead us toward our goals: self-esteem for those previously not reflected in the mirror, and important enlightenment for those who, for too long, have seen only themselves in that mirror; all leading toward the celebration of living in our multicultural society.

However, one must begin with specific books. How do we recognize authenticity in children's books about African-Americans? It is difficult for reviewers who are not African-Americans to evaluate authenticity unless and until they have been immersed in a large body of authentic works, because the African-American experience is so varied and manifested in so many different ways. Furthermore, we must acknowledge that reader response is also important in defining authenticity. We cannot ignore what a book does to a reader in our quest for authenticity, for genuineness. Truth is at least partly a matter of feeling. What is it about a book that makes us say, "Yes, yes, that's how it is"? We know it is true because we feel it, deep down.

Some years ago I read *Roll of Thunder, Hear My Cry*, and I knew. I did not grow up in Mississippi, I never had to undergo any kind of prejudice like that the Logan family experienced, but the story struck a chord, a wrenching chord. I knew Mildred Taylor was writing my history. A Euro-American in a suburban school might not know any of the history, but that reader would *feel* with Cassie and Little Man in their hurt, and would be touched by Jeremy's efforts to be their friend. This experience could make a difference in how such a reader might respond to real life African-Americans. In Taylor's stories of a particular time and place, the plight of Blacks becomes imaginable, tangible, and true because her art evokes feelings. An authentic experience is possible for the reader. Of course, such an experience is authentic, real, and genuine to different degrees and in different ways, depending on what the reader brings to the book.

I recently read *Baseball in April*—wonderful! I have only two Mexican-American friends, but yet, after reading the book, I feel as though I do know some teenagers who live in Fresno. Something about the portrayal of family relationships reflected my own teenage years and those of my daughters. A universality of experience pervades those stories in the particularity of characters and setting; this is one way to recognize authenticity in a work of literature. Readers from the culture will know that it is true, will identify, and be affirmed, and readers from another culture will feel that it is true, will identify, and learn something of value, sometimes merely that there are more similarities than differences among us.

If the purpose of literature is to liberate, the purpose of authentic multicultural literature is to help liberate us from all the preconceived stereotypical hang-ups that imprison us within narrow boundaries. Non-majority readers will be liberated from the invisibility imposed from without, the invisibility that says loudly to children, "You don't count."

In writing about authenticity in books depicting African-American experience, I want to consider how and why I have begun to write about this experience. In the process, I would like to offer some thoughts about who is an African-American and *who* can create authentic African-American literature for children.

We are fortunate in 1991. We now need more than two hands, more than ten fingers, to count significant African-American authors and illustrators; publishers seem to be paying attention. However, this is not really cause for rejoicing. Children's book publishing has become an enormous business, and the small percentage of books depicting non-majority experience written and illustrated by people from that experience is appalling; at best, it is one percent of all the children's books being published. More African-American authors for children have recently appeared, but of the 51 books by African-American authors published last year, 11 were published by small presses. (Thank heavens for Just Us Books!) What does this say about the commitment of the approximately 64 members of the Children's Book Council? This seeming flurry of publishing of multicultural books could be just another bubble, another flash in the pan, although the spreading of the whole language movement is encouraging. Perhaps as the need for more tradebooks in the schools increases, there will be greater awareness of the reality of our pluralistic culture and of the fact that books do provide an essential experience for living multiculturally. But we must not cease to be wary, those of us who care. This has happened before.

Indeed, there are now more books authentically portraying African-American experience, but there are also more books about African-Americans not written by Blacks, and there are other books by non-Blacks that include some major characters who are Black. Are these books authentic? What about authors like Cynthia Voigt, Bruce Brooks, Bette Greene, Ouida Sebestyen? What about Lois Lowry? What about these books? The basic question, the important question, which I continually hear is: "For a book about African-Americans to be authentic, does the writer have to be Black?" I say, "Yes. Yes, you have to be African-American." Then they'll ask, "What about Ezra Jack Keats or James Collier?" I will still say, "To write an authentic book reflecting another cultural experience, you have to be of that culture." They'll ask slyly, "Do you have to be Chinese to write about Chinese people?" And I'll answer, "Yes." They'll respond, "Well, Jean Fritz wrote about China!" and I'll reply, "Jean Fritz *is* Chinese. If she isn't, she's pretty close." Jean Fritz grew up in China, knows Chinese people well, and she wrote about herself in China. I believe she could write authentic fiction, perhaps, about Chinese characters. So although I say that someone has to be African-American to write about African-Americans, it is *possible* for someone who may not be so identified on a birth certificate to do so, but it is *not* easy. If that person is emotionally and experientially African-American, if he or she sees something desirable, something worthy of imitating in being African-American, if this person is aware in his or her bones of the intertwining of history and geography and biology and blood and sweat and life so that he or she can indeed feel, to some degree, African-American, then, I think it is possible. Isn't Arnold Adoff pretty close to being Black?

What about those of us who are identified as African-American on our birth certificate and through our culturation? How can we define African-American? Most of all, it is the infinite variety. That is the joy of being African-American; it is in the blend and in the bonding that transcends class and skin color and geography and time. This shows up in our books.

Where do we get this loyalty to family, this spirituality and deep affinity for religion, this camaraderie, this *joie de vivre*, this respect for older people, this hope in the young, this love of music, this sense of poetry, this sense of humor, this passion for justice, this feeling for the group, this capacity to survive, and this loyalty to America? It is in the blend of experiences, of life, of history, and tradition. It is Africa and America and the historical memory of a people that make up African-Americans. It is multicultural and it needs to be described in more and more books for children.

African-Americans are basically Americans, and our lives are American lives reflecting the good and the less good of the dominant culture. Whatever was purely African has been absorbed into the new blend, the new people that we are always becoming. At the same time, the dominant society is also becoming inevitably, in subtle or not so subtle ways, more African-American. (Everybody's rappin' now!) There is something African that pervades the lives of Euro-Americans. Americans have been a multicultural people from the first, and I'm not referring to the melting pot theory which denigrated the culture of the home places. (African-Americans never did melt.) A multicultural society is evolving in which people are free to tell their own story. Children need to hear and read these stories.

I want to help to tell that story of the historic reality. It is what I was trying to do in *Chita's Christmas Tree* and *Aunt Flossie's Hats (and Crab Cakes Later)* and *The Train to Lulu's*. Writing authentically for children of the African-American experience means creating many different books. It is a vast and varied experience, rich and wonderful, and it belongs to all of us. Mildred Pitts Walter tells children about Black cowboys in *Justin and the Best Biscuits in the World*—who would know about them if she hadn't told her story? In *Fast Sam, Cool Clyde, and Stuff*, Walter Dean Myers shows that there are kids in Harlem who have caring, concerned families, ambitions, and don't have to succumb to the drug culture around them. Virginia Hamilton tells of a Black family who lived around the turn of the century in *The*

Bells of Christmas. These people worked hard, maybe as teachers, maybe some (like my great-uncle Jimmy, who is mentioned in *Aunt Flossie's Hats*) had a grocery store. They led active community lives. They supported their church, saved their money, aspired for higher education for their children, and believed in this country, all the while living within the segregated system. All Americans need to know that the history of these people is part of the history of all of us. African-American writers have the necessary historical memory to write it down. How does one write authentically as an African-American, or as a member of any group? One writes from what one knows, one writes from who one is. I would like to share a bit of my own multicultural history.

by Elizabeth Fitzgerald Howard · illustrated by Floyd Cooper

From *Chita's Christmas Tree* by *Elizabeth Fitzgerald Howard. Illus. Copyright © 1989 by Floyd Cooper. Reproduced by Permission of Bradbury Press, an Affiliate of Macmillan, Inc.*

When I was a little girl, I lived in a castle at the top of a high hill. There were 32 steps scattered along a slowly ascending lawn. Near the top of the lawn, there was a rock garden planted pink and purple, and around the side was a shady dell. Goblins lived here among the lilies of the valley and the irises. In back, there was a large outcropping of rock. My sister and I could climb this rock and keep watch to warn of marauders approaching from the direction of Brighton High School. Inside the castle, there lived a witch. She was large and forbidding, and her name was Mrs. Ella Ford. Other inhabitants of the castle were two wizards and a dragon lady. They had small cells on the second floor and green eye shades. I lived on the third floor, as did my parents and my sister. We were princesses, Babs and I. My mother was the queen and my father was the king. From the royal nursery, you could see far, far over the kingdom, even to Harvard Stadium. We could peer toward the horizon and call, "Sister Anne, Sister Anne, do you see anyone coming?"

I did live in a castle, but it was a Black rooming house in a white neighborhood in Allston, Massachusetts. It was Depression time. Mrs. Ella Ford took in African-American graduate students who were attending some of the universities around Boston. My parents and my sister and I lived in the attic. My father, the king, worked for the WPA, and my mother, the queen, painted greeting cards. My sister and I played with the peasant children in the neighborhood. They were all white. We played with Ruth and Muriel whose parents forbade them to go near "those colored children." They came every day and played in our attic room or in the backyard. Who could resist a castle and two princesses?

On Sundays, my parents often took us to Roxbury to visit with the children of their friends, Negro children. This was always fun. But most of our days, we just played stealthily with Ruth and Muriel. My other friends, with whom I spent many hours, were also white. They lived in books, and their names were Jo and Meg and Beth and Amy, and Maida, and Elsie Dinsmore, and Nancy Drew, plus all of the people who lived in Asgard and Mount Olympus and the Lang fairytale books and Hawthorne's *Wonder-Book*. I truly identified with all of them, and with Shirley Temple, too. Did I ever wonder why none of the book people were my color? I don't think I ever even thought about it. Would my sense of self have been different if Virginia Hamilton or Walter Myers or Mildred Pitts Walter had been writing then?

Summers were special. On the Sunday after school closed, my sister and I took the train to Lulu's. Lulu was our great aunt, an elementary teacher, childless, who lived in a house in the country outside of Baltimore. For five summers, Babs and I were rocked in the bosom of an extended family who we might not have really known very well otherwise. Here everyone was colored, uncles and aunts and cousins in all shades, from pale pink Aunt Eva to deep ebony Aunt Erma. We knew we belonged, and we learned here something else about being Black. We learned about the colored end of Sparrow's Beach (the sand here was rough); we learned about sitting in the balcony at the movies; and that Uncle Howard had to buy a hat that didn't fit him because he had presumed to try it on. But all of this didn't matter much to us. There was plenty of love all around.

THE TRAIN TO LULU'S

By Elizabeth Fitzgerald Howard / Illustrated by Robert Casilla

Illustration by Robert Casilla. From Train to Lulu's by Elizabeth Fitzgerald Howard. Illus. Copyright © 1988 by Robert Casilla.. Reproduced by permission of Bradbury Press, an Affiliate of Macmillan, Inc.

A good thing happened for my own identity just as I was almost a teenager. Lulu moved to

Boston, lived with us at Mrs. Ella Ford's for a year, and then we moved to Roxbury to an apartment in a Black neighborhood. It was wonderful! I was just beginning to be slightly aware of boys. Not old enough for parties or dates but old enough to sit on the front steps on summer nights and play Red Rover or Categories. I was definitely and most happily colored and aware that it was pretty nice.

Then Lulu bought our house in Brookline in the middle of a Jewish middle-class neighborhood and I had to transfer—with weeping and wailing and gnashing of teeth—to Brookline High School. Not only was I once again the only African-American in the school, I was also one of two non-Jewish students in all my college prep classes. In my neighborhood, I became aware of Jewish refugees from Hitler's Europe. Across the street, Mrs. Meyer kept a kosher boarding house and I helped her daughter, Johanna, who was in my class, wait table at dinner time. One old gentleman offered to help me with my German if I would help him with English. I belonged at Mrs. Meyer's, and because I was a good student I belonged at Brookline High School, but I didn't belong in the dating and football game scene. Anyway, my mother said that books and boys never mix.

I was admitted to Radcliffe College and plunged into another whole culture, the extreme WASP dormitory life. My cousin, Chita, paid for my dormitory room, and my Aunt Flossie paid half of my tuition. The rest was scholarship. I was the only African-American in my class of 200. If I didn't fit in, if anyone objected to my being there, I never noticed it. I loved everybody. I ran for and won offices and sang in the choral society, and I put studying on a lower priority level, as casual as my debutante acquaintances about grades. Who was I becoming? Socially, I knew I was a Negro. I dated only the handful of Black college youths from the schools around Boston; some came from the South. After awhile, I met a young African-American graduate student from Iowa (who ever heard of a Negro from Iowa?). His father had gone out of South Carolina, taken the train as far north as his money would go, settled in Des Moines and graduated from Drake Law School. His mother's family had arrived in Iowa Territory in covered wagons and settled on a large farm before Iowa was a state.

We got married and lived happily ever after. Our life together has continued to be multicultural, from the Brandeis University Campus to the Philippines with the Peace Corps where I almost became Filipino, and was sometimes mistaken for one. When it was time to return home after two enriching years I cried, and wondered why I had to leave. I asked myself about the idea of world citizenship. Shortly after we returned home, our third daughter was born, Laura Ligaya. Her middle name means "joy" in Tagalog, commemorating that special time.

And then, Lord, the 60s! We came home from the Philippines to find the Civil Rights struggle in full strength. Our identity as Black Americans was sharpened as we worked for school integration, neighborhood integration, church integration.

While living in Milwaukee we organized a freedom school. Later, we lived in St. Louis, and then we moved to Pittsburgh, where we have been for the last 20 years (for 12 of these years I spent two nights each week of the school year in West Virginia). We have not traveled much lately, but the world has come to us as students from various parts of Africa have lived semester after semester in our house, and as our children have been involved in international exchange arrangements with friends in Bogota, Colombia.

We were fortunate to live in Africa for a year. En route, as we deplaned for a stop in Cairo, our first footprint on African soil, our middle daughter, Susan, exclaimed, "Africa, Africa, the Motherland!" and almost kissed the sandy runway. Our African home was Maiduguri, in northeastern Nigeria, an area of primarily Muslim Hausa and Kanuri people. We became accustomed to the call to prayer, to the wonders of the market, to the harmattan, that cool desert wind that settles sand everywhere. I wanted to collect folktales for possible retelling and taped stories in several places, most notably, in the little village of Dalori. I imagined that my ancestors had come from that village. In a very real way, we felt Kanuri. As a result, I have been reluctant to try to make anything unauthentic of those Nigerian folktales.

This is one African-American story. There is more in the history of those people in Baltimore whom I have celebrated in my books. But this story of mine is not unique. Being African-American means having stories. We all have our Aunt Flossies and our Cousin Chitas and our Great Aunt Lulus, who have given so much and who have made us what we are. These stories are waiting to be told. We desperately need more African-American writers, and I would like to encourage you to find the stories and write them down. We need to fill in the gaps. We need to aim toward developing an authentic, real body of African-American children's literature. It is a big task. How many Phoebe Yehs and Ana Nuncios are there in the major publishing houses? Who is making decisions about what will be available for the growing numbers of non-European Americans? Of course, the editors are not the only ones responsible. What is happening with the books that we have now? Are the teachers and the librarians truly aware of the impact that they can have on young people with these books? How can we mount an effort significant enough to be sure that teachers and librarians in preparation and those already in the schools know these books, so that they will demand these books for our children? The children's book industry has a mandate to develop an authentic African-American literature for all children. Our future depends on our understanding each other, appreciating each other, and children's books have a crucial role in making us ready for that future.

Notes:

1. Greenfield, "Honey, I Love", [1]. Excerpted from "Honey, I Love" from *Honey, I Love and Other Poems.* Copyright © 1978 by Eloise Greenfield. Illustrations copyright © 1978 by Diane and Leo Dillon. Reprinted by permission of HarperCollins Publishers.

Works Cited:

Greenfield, Eloise. *Honey, I Love and Other Love Poems.* Illustrated by Leo and Diane Dillon. New York: Thomas Y. Crowell, 1978.

Hamilton, Virginia. *The Bells of Christmas.* Illustrated by Lambert Davis. San Diego: Harcourt Brace Jovanovich, 1989.

Howard, Elizabeth Fitzgerald. *Aunt Flossie's Hats (and Crab Cakes Later).* Illustrated by James Ransome. New York: Clarion, 1991.

———. *Chita's Christmas Tree.* Illustrated by Floyd Cooper. New York: Bradbury, 1989.

———. *The Train To Lulu's.* Illustrated by Robert Casilla. New York: Bradbury, 1988.

Myers, Walter Dean. *Fast Sam, Cool Clyde, and Stuff.* New York: Viking, 1975.

Soto, Gary. *Baseball in April and Other Stories.* San Diego: Harcourt Brace Jovanovich, 1990.

Taylor, Mildred D. *Roll of Thunder, Hear My Cry.* New York: Dial, 1976.

Walter, Mildred Pitts. *Justin and the Best Biscuits in the World.* Illustrated by Catherine Stock. New York: Lothrop, Lee & Shepard, 1986.

Bibliography of Books Written by Elizabeth Fitzgerald Howard

America as Story: Historical Fiction for Secondary Schools. Chicago: American Library Association, 1988.

Aunt Flossie's Hats (and Crab Cakes Later). Illustrated by James Ransome. New York: Clarion, 1991.

Chita's Christmas Tree. Illustrated by Floyd Cooper. New York: Bradbury, 1989.

The Train to Lulu's. Illustrated by Robert Casilla. New York: Bradbury, 1988.

1492 - 1992 From an American Indian Perspective

Doris Seale

From the beginning of speech, human beings have told stories to their children—to amuse them, and to teach them the ways of their people. As the structure of Western society became more formalized and more rigid, so did the instruction. The first writing for children was for purposes of indoctrination, and the truth is, much of it still is. Even fiction, even picture books for very young children, tend to carry messages about things that some people think they need to know—depending upon their motivation, to become acquiescent members of society, or to grow and thrive, socially and spiritually as well as physically. This is not *necessarily* a "bad" thing . . . . Only: children believe that what they read in books is the truth . . . .

Children's books about the history and condition of my people fall basically into two categories, whether fiction or nonfiction: 1) The historical, in which a superior culture triumphs, with the more "liberal" writers admitting that this may have had its more unfortunate aspects for the Native population, and 2) Contemporary works, in which Native people have failed lamentably to "adapt" to modern civilization and can only achieve resolution by giving up their primitive ways. In fiction, whether historical or contemporary, the role of the Native person is most often as friend to the white protagonist so that she or he may learn a valuable lesson in her or his maturation process, or so that the author may make some point about that aforementioned superior culture.

I have been talking for a very long time and with increasing frustration about the books. Now I will focus on the truth that is *not* in them.

Doris Seale, who is Santee, Cree, and white, is a children's librarian at the Brookline Public Library in Massachusetts and the co-author of Books Without Bias: Through Indian Eyes. *She is a member of the Native American Advisory Board of the Children's Museum of Boston. She has written numerous book reviews and articles for the* Interracial Books for Children Bulletin *and has contributed poetry to* Fireweed *and* Gathering of Spirit, *two collections of writings by Native American women.*

Books Without Bias: Through Indian Eyes, *formerly published by Oyate Press, is now available from New Society Publishers.*

What I write here is but a small part of the story of our lives in 500 years, only the tops of mountains. These things happened to people of flesh and blood. This is no long-ago thing. We are here, now, living in your midst, but you do not see us.

The whole western world is throwing a party next year. They say they are celebrating the "discovery" of the "new world." The chairman of the United States Jubilee Committee is John Gaudie, a real estate developer. Well, that seems appropriate . . . . He says that Columbus's achievement is "what the American dream is all about."[1] The literature relating to the Quincentenary is already voluminous, and growing. Most of it is written from the assumption that colonization is the only way to advance "civilization." Columbus's voyage is taken as a metaphor for the continued success of Western Civilization. While the more liberal may admit that the conquest of the Americas had its negative aspects for the indigenous population, at least at first, taken as a whole, it is seen as a Good Thing. Some do also use the word "civilizations" when referring to the Aztecs and the Incas, but for the rest of it, the western hemisphere is believed to have been wilderness, just awaiting development. The theme will be, the wild overcome by a superior culture and technology, as is right and proper; conquest, colonization, civilization.

Columbus, eh.

Although no one knows what he looked like, he is described as having "keen blue eyes;" tall, with red hair — really more like an Anglo-Saxon, don't you know.

He wasn't the first.

And it is not true that he was the only person in Europe in 1492 who knew the world was round, either. While the knowledge of the ancient world was lost to Europeans during the dark ages, contact with the Islamic world had, by the time of Columbus, restored much of it, and it is doubtful that there were many educated people, at least, who believed that the world was flat. They also knew how big it was, which is one reason nobody had tried going East by sailing West. One reason that Columbus so firmly believed he could do it was that he also firmly believed that the world was really only three-quarters as big as everybody else said it was. He never would have made it, if not for the northeast trade winds that blew him over, and the westerlies that brought him back. To his dying day, he insisted that he had found Asia. Everybody knows that. What may not be so well-known — and this was to have the direst consequences for "*Los Indios*" — was that even for that bigoted age, Columbus was an extreme religious fanatic. What is also not well-known, although it is right there, in his own hand, in the diaries, is that he was no unwilling bystander to the slaughter of the local population.

It is a matter of record that Columbus and his men were received with friendship wherever they went. Their response? "To win their friendship . . . I gave some of them red caps, glass beads, and many other little things . . . these pleased them very much and they became very friendly. They willingly traded everything they owned . . . . They would make fine servants . . . . these people are totally unskilled in arms, as your majesties will learn from seven whom I had captured and taken aboard . . . . Should your majesties command it, all the inhabitants could be taken away to Castile, or made slaves on the island. With fifty men we could subjugate them all and make them do whatever we want."[2]

Some of those people had little gold ornaments in their ears and noses . . . .

Bartolomé de las Casas, originally an admirer of Columbus, came to the Indies and wrote about what he saw there in his *History of the Indies*: Indians, treated "not as beasts, for beasts are treated properly at times, but like excrement in a public square."[3] And, Columbus was "at the *beginning* (emphasis mine) of [the] ill usage afflicted upon them."[4]

The people who, "When you ask for something they have, they never say no,"[5] the people described by Columbus as generous, innocent, and comely, had become, by the second voyage, "savages," suitable for slavery and extortion, because he was in trouble. Columbus had consistently promised his backers, the Spanish sovereigns, untold wealth from the Indies. He was a terrible liar. "These islands are richer than I know or can say . . . . In this island of Hispaniola I have taken possession of a large town, which is very well situated both for the gold fields and for communication with the mainland and the land of the great Khan . . ."[6] There were, of course, no gold fields, so in 1495, when a shipment was due home, and reality was about to catch up with him, Columbus decided to fill his ships up with slaves. Fifteen hundred people were rounded up. While waiting for shipment, they were kept in pens guarded by dogs. The ships had space only for 500, so only the best specimens were kept. Columbus let his men choose from the rest as many as they liked for their personal slaves. The rejects were simply kicked out. So great had their terror been while held captive that, when they were released, in the words of one witness, "They rushed in all directions like lunatics, women dropping and abandoning infants in the rush, running for miles without stopping . . . ."[7]

But, gold Columbus had promised and, sooner or later, gold he would have to produce. De las Casas describes for us the system devised for procuring what little alluvial gold there was on Hispaniola. Every person 14 years of age and older was required to bring in a hawk's bill full of gold dust every three months. Chiefs were responsible for ten times as much. Those who could not comply had their hands cut off and were allowed to bleed to death. Those who tried to escape were hunted down with dogs. The only army the people were ever able to raise was quickly destroyed and all prisoners hanged, or burned, or both.

De las Casas tells us that low, wide gallows were built on which the captives could be hung with their feet just above the ground. Under their feet, slow-burning fires were built from green wood. The executions were done in lots of 13, "in memory of our Redeemer and the 12 apostles."[8] Chiefs and nobles were burned to death on grids made of iron rods. When a captain ordered that they be strangled before burning because their cries kept him awake, the executioner pinned their tongues with sticks so that they could not cry out and "roasted them slowly, as he liked."[9] It was at this time that the mass suicides began.

In a two year period, half the population of Hispaniola died, either by their own hands or at the hands of the Spanish. The estimates vary from 100,000 to a half a million, but by 1515 there were less than 10,000 people left. In another 25 years, the Arawaks and Tainos had ceased to exist as viable populations.

In 1615, an English slave ship, skippered by a Captain Hunt, visited a town on the Massachusetts coast called Patuxet by its inhabitants. Hunt kidnapped a number of the local populace and left smallpox behind. The disease ravaged the Wampanoag nation for four years and took a severe toll on the nearby Massachusetts. This plague was regarded by the pilgrim fathers as having been a gift from their God to clear the way for them. They called it The Wonderful Preparation [of] the Lord Jesus Christ by his Providence for His People's Abode in the Western World. They were particularly grateful because the disease had claimed "chiefly young men and children, the very seeds of increase."[10]

On the Massachusetts shore, the newcomers had been received, as was the case everywhere, with kindness and the hand of friendship. By the time of the sachem Massasoit's death, the English abuses had turned friendship to hatred. When Massasoit's son, called Alexander by the colonists, died in their hands, his brother, Metacomet, known to white people as King Philip, took up arms against them. At that time, there were 50,000 white settlers in New England, but in spite of the odds against him, Metacomet was initially successful, although he was defeated in the end. His principle chiefs were killed, and his wife and son captured and sold into slavery in the West Indies. After they had killed Metacomet, the white men cut off his head and took it to Plymouth, where it was hung on display for 25 years.

The white nation grew apace, and everywhere the white people went they carried their diseases and their belief that anything they saw that they wanted should be theirs. While the coastal peoples were suffering the avarice and religious persecution of the English, who had come to their shores seeking religious freedom, to the north and west of them the peoples of the original Iroquois Five Nations were trying to maintain some sort of balance between the English and the French.

By the beginning of the eighteenth century, the practice of offering bounties for Indian scalps had become common. An incident in the Pennsylvania village of

Conestoga was typical. On one December night, bounty hunters earned $1,500 by killing and scalping three old men, two women, and a boy. Some of the white residents of the town, fearing for the lives of the Indians in their employ, rounded them up with their families and put them in the town jail for their safety. The bounty hunters broke into the jail and killed everybody. An English regiment stationed in the town took no action.

Defeat of the French by the British in the French and Indian War left the English a number of nations to deal with in the newly acquired lands: Shawnee, Miami, Kickapoo, Potawatomie, Mesquakie, Chippewa, Illinois, Ottawa, and Delaware. In the first known instance of germ warfare, Lord Jeffrey Amherst deliberately sent blankets taken from smallpox victims to these people when he grew impatient with their intractability. This was only one of many similar incidents.

As a result of Pontiac's so-called rebellion, the British made an official line of demarcation between Indian and colonial territories. The colonists were infuriated and had no intention of respecting it. At the time of the American Revolution both George Washington and Patrick Henry had extensive holdings in Indian territory. Daniel Boone was instrumental in acquiring most of what is Kentucky for the Transylvania Company. Benjamin Franklin, as American representative to the Crown, was able to use his office to help the Walpole Company take over 20 million acres of Indian land, all of it well beyond the Appalachian boarder that had been guaranteed to the Indians.

Unfortunately for them, many Indian nations sided with the British during the revolution because of the way they had been treated by the colonists. The Continental Congress "declared that the victory over England left the Indian nations a defeated enemy with no more rights than their 'conquerors' might please to give them." By siding with the English, the Indians "lost all right to expect recognition of the territorial treaties."[11] In the long run, it probably did not make much of a difference.

After their war, the new nation forged ahead with the business of Indian control, called "Building a Nation" and, later, "Manifest Destiny." Ohio Territory was vigorously defended by Miami, Shawnee, and Delaware. In 1794, the U.S. sent 3,600 army regulars under General Anthony Wayne into Indian territory. At Fallen Timbers, Blue Jacket and his 1,400 were soundly defeated by this force. General Wayne celebrated by burning every Native village he could find. Land was ceded, of course, and almost immediately the Americans began pushing against the new boundaries.

After the soldiers came the missionaries. Some, no doubt, were genuinely motivated. But they have never been content to merely save the souls of their savage brethren, supposing that were necessary. The cultural baggage of the

Americans included an ethnocentrism so extreme that they haven't yet gotten over it. To this day, historians explain the destruction of Native life as simply the inevitable consequences of contact with a superior culture.

Had the conquerors been content with the spoils of victory, it would have been disaster enough. Although, in fact, what was waged against the Native population was not formally declared war, with its declarations, treaty terms more-or-less-honorably kept, and rules about the treatment of prisoners and noncombatants. The Americans would not be content merely with winning; cultures must be destroyed as well. From the California missions to the missionaries of the Protestant sects, it was believed that the heathen must not only be saved, they must also be "civilized." Nobody knows for sure how many people died under the system of slavery instituted by the California missions, but of the Yana Nation (to pick just one) a population of 2,000 to 3,000 in 1492 became 12 by 1928. Some nations didn't make it at all.

In any case, everywhere on the American frontier soldiers and whiskey traders were followed by missionaries Red Jacket, Seneca, had this to say of so-called "educated" Indians: "What have we here? You are neither a white man nor an Indian; for heaven's sake, tell us, what are you?" (This was a tragedy inflicted upon many thousands of our young people, up until this day.) To a missionary who tried to point out to him the error of his ways, he said, "If you white people murdered 'the Savior,' make it up among yourselves. We had nothing to do with it. If he had come among us we would have treated him better."[12] We shall see how much good becoming "civilized" did the Indians.

Cherokee, Creek, Chickasaw, Choctaw, and Seminole peoples were referred to as the Five Civilized Tribes, meaning they were deserving of respect on the white man's terms. In 1826, the Cherokee alone owned "22,000 head of cattle, 7,600 horses, 46,000 pigs, 726 looms, 2,488 spinning wheels, 172 wagons, 2,943 plows, 10 sawmills, 31 grain mills, 62 blacksmith [shops], 8 cotton machines, 18 schools, and 18 ferries."[13] There were two problems with this: one, the Cherokee were willing to learn from the white man, but not to learn to become brown-white people; the other, all this prosperity was driving the white people around them nuts. By now most people have at least a general idea of what happened to these people; of how they fought removal and lost, even though what was done to them was completely illegal by the white man's own laws. The Choctaw were the first to go, forced out in the middle of the winter of 1832, from Mississippi to Oklahoma. Many were barefoot, all were starving. One blanket was allotted to each family. Exact figures are unavailable, but it is known that of the Cherokee alone, at least 4,000 died. Van Buren, president at the time, told Congress, "The measures authorized by the Congress have had the happiest effects . . . . the Cherokees have emigrated without any apparent reluctance . . . ."[14] By the end of the removal period, around 1850, more than 100,000 people from 28 different nations had been deported west of the Mississippi. We know that at least 30,000 died.

Having accomplished the "Indian Removal" east of the Mississippi, the Americans now began to cast their eyes across what they had assured the Native population was to be a "permanent boundary" between white and Indian lands. All along this boundary you could find traders, whiskey peddlers, and the riffraff of the "Westward Movement," as well as soldiers and churchmen. They brought smallpox, cholera, measles, and venereal diseases which raged throughout the Nations in devastating epidemics. In 1842 the Oregon Trail opened. From then on it was the usual tale of chicanery and double dealing. In 1851, the Santee were tricked into signing away all their lands in Minnesota, Iowa, and the Dakota Territory. They were allowed to keep a 20-mile wide strip along the Missouri River; in 1858, half of that was taken away by Senate decree. Factionalism was encouraged by Americans and developed into the schism between traditionals and hang-around-the-fort Indians from which we suffer to this day. When, in 1862, having finally had enough, the Santees struck back in what came to be called "Little Crow's War," they were defeated. Little Crow refused to surrender and escaped to Canada. On a horse raid into Minnesota, he and his son were surprised while picking blueberries by two white hunters and shot. "Minnesota was paying a scalp bounty of 25 dollars then, but when the authorities found whose scalp they had, the two hunters received an added 500 dollars. Little Crow's scalp—as well his skull—was preserved and exhibited in St. Paul."[15] On December 26, 38 Santees were hanged at Mankato by decree of President Abraham Lincoln, the Great Emancipator. It is told how they sang their death songs and tried to hold hands to give each other courage.

In 1864, a party of Cheyenne under Black Kettle were camped at Sand Creek, Colorado. On the morning of November 28, Colonel Chivington led 700 men armed with Howitzers in an attack on the sleeping Cheyenne. The sworn testimony of Robert Bent, a guide who was present, states: "When we came in sight of camp I saw the American flag waving and heard Black Kettle tell the Indians to stand around the flag, and there they huddled—men, women, and children . . . . I also saw a white flag raised. These flags were in so conspicuous a position that they must have been seen . . . . I think there were 600 Indians in all. I think there were about 35 braves and some old men, about 60 in all. [The rest were women and children.] All fought well . . . . I revisited the battleground one month afterwards; saw the remains of a great many . . . but a number had been eaten by wolves and dogs . . . . Everyone I saw dead was scalped. I saw one squaw cut open with an unborn child . . . . I saw the body of White Antelope with the privates cut off, and I heard a soldier say he was going to make a tobacco pouch out of them. I saw one squaw whose privates had been cut out . . . ." [16]

When Chivington was reprimanded at the Congressional investigation, at which the above testimony was given, for the toll in women and, especially, children, he said, "Kill 'em all, large and small. Nits make lice." After the Sand Creek massacre, many Cheyennes joined the Dakotas in their resistance.

The treaty of 1868 banned all trade on the Platte River and required all Indians to live on reservations west of the Missouri. An edgy sort of peace ensued. The treaty guaranteed that white men would stay away from Indian lands—again.

In 1870 there were rumors of gold in the Big Horns, and the whites demanded that this territory be opened up to them. In 1873, Lieutenant General George Armstrong Custer was transferred to the area with his 7th Cavalry. I know that this man is still a hero to many Americans, and we are supposed to have respected him and called him Yellow Hair and all that. Here's what he was really called, Woman Killer, and none of that crap about Son of the Morning Star, excuse me.

One of the first things Custer did was invade Lakota territory with a party of surveyors for the Northern Pacific Railroad. The following year he came back with an expeditionary force of 1,200 men. His aim this time was the Black Hills, and his party included newspaper correspondents to report his exploits, scientists, and white gold miners. Red Cloud and Spotted Tail protested to Washington; the answer was a delegation authorized to buy the Black Hills. A word about the Black Hills. This is one of the most sacred sites on earth, the center of the world, the dwelling place of sacred beings, a place where young men went to receive visions, where spiritual leaders went to seek counsel. The Black Hills were not for sale then, they are not for sale now. They were never ceded. They belong to us, we belong to them.

This delegation made everybody very nervous. More than 20,000 Lakota, Cheyenne, and Arapaho people camped around the counsel site. They were determined that this time, at least, the whites were not going to be able to say that they had made a deal with the whole nation just by getting a few "friendlies" drunk enough to sign a piece of paper. The delegation went back to Washington recommending that Congress simply pay no attention to what the Indians wanted. The government should decide what payment the Indians should get and present it to them as a *fait accompli*; then send in the army to enforce it.

In the winter of 1875 the order went out for all Indians to come into the agencies. There were skirmishes into the spring and summer as more and more people left the reservation to join the resistance. I doubt it is necessary to say very much about the Custer fight. It was the most expensive victory in history, one paid for dearly 14 years later at Wounded Knee. A victory still being paid for by the Northern Plains peoples, who are the most hated and maltreated people in North America—that's a nearly thing.

By the 1880s it was almost over. Joseph had surrendered, after leading his people, including women, children, and the old, on a retreat of some 1,300 miles, harassed all the way by three separate armies. Geronimo surrendered in 1886, beginning a 27-year term, along with 340 of his people, as prisoner-of-war at Fort Marion (Florida), Mount Vernon Barracks (Alabama), and Fort Sill (Oklahoma). Although he was promised a place in his original homeland, Geronimo was never allowed to go home. He died, and is buried, at Fort Sill.

Historians of the period are fond of saying that Geronimo was one of the finest guerilla fighters of all time. They do not often tell that, beginning with the murder of his mother, wife, and three children, he lived to see all his children dead whether by violence or from disease and the horrible living conditions of his long captivity.

There was not a nation that had not suffered from the upheaval and displacement caused by the relentless advance of the white men. Some of the peoples who were sent, either as prisoners-of-war or during removal, to Oklahoma (known as "Indian territory") were: Kickapoo, Tonkawa, Commanche, Chiracahua Apache, Creek, Choctaw, Chickasaw, Cherokee, Shawnee, Potawatomie, Mesquakie, Nez Perce, Ponca, Pawnee, and Modoc. The Navajos—8,500 starving men, women, and children—had endured their own death march, the Long Walk to Bosque Redondo (Fort Sumner) in New Mexico. The final event, what has been called the last "battle" of the "Indian wars," was the massacre of 350 of Big Foot's band of Miniconjous at Wounded Knee Creek on December 29, 1890. Twenty-six U.S. soldiers who participated were given the Congressional Medal of Honor for their efforts.

The years following saw the suppression of everything Indian. Everything that would sustain us was forbidden—the Sun Dance, the Potlatch, the Kiva. No trace of Native religion was to be allowed to survive. In the interests of "assimilation" and "acculturation" (more respectable terms than genocide) Native children were taken from their parents to be "educated." Since the actual aim of this education was the destruction of the family and traditional life-ways, most were not allowed to return home for several years. At the white boarding schools the children were beaten for a variety of things: for speaking their own languages, for forming friendships with other children, for trying to protect each other, for "insolence," for any infraction of the rules, no matter how slight; beaten for the first time in their lives, since most Native people thought that anyone who would strike a child had to be insane. They were taught that their religions were "savage" superstitions, that their arts, customs, and life-ways were pathetic excuses for a culture, that white "civilization" was superior in every way. At the same time, they were taught nothing that would usefully prepare them for actual assimilation into white society; that was not the intent. Girls learned domestic arts, boys learned manual labor. Destination? Servants to white people.

As a result, generations of our children were totally unfitted for any kind of life. Although the Cherokees had clearly demonstrated that Native people were as capable of using the tools of white "civilization" as were the whites themselves, these poor little misfits were taken as proof that the Indian wasn't capable of learning; a catch-22 situation from which we have as yet to entirely escape.

Even before Wounded Knee, plans for the further destruction of the Native land base found expression in the 1887 General Allotment Act (the Dawes Act). The rationalization was that it would give Indians pride of ownership and encourage them to become good farmers. In actuality it was designed to destroy the reservation system and put an end to tribal relations based on traditions of generosity and sharing. The Act designated 160 acres of land for each head of the family, 80 acres for single adults, and 40 acres for minors. And—here we come to the heart of it—whatever was left over would be sold to whites. By this and similar methods, the 138 million acres owned by native people in 1877 was reduced by the 1960s to 50 million acres. The poverty, disease, disunity, loss of language and tribal tradition that the People have endured until now are not the inevitable result of cultural conflict and "interchange," but of deliberate policies. Since day one, this nation has sought an end to the existence of the indigenous population, although often calling it by other names: relocation, termination, acculturation. Few politicians are now as outspoken as was Benjamin Franklin when he said that rum should be regarded as an agent of Providence "to extirpate these savages in order to make room for the cultivators of the earth." [17]

Where are we now? Still here, oddly enough. There is a curious phenomenon: now that we are safely tamed, now that they own the whole country and see little possibility of their version of the story being called into question, Americans have become fascinated with Indians. Not around reservations, of course, but that is another story. In the 1991 *Subject Guide to Books in Print*, there are 46 pages listing books about Indians. Not a whole lot of them have been *written* by Indians. . . .[18] Thousands of anthropologists have spent enjoyable summers with, in Floyd Westerman's words, their "feathered friends," and built reputations and lucrative careers on what they learned from them. Hundreds of little white boys learn to play Indian at Boy Scout camps; thousands of little white girls participate in "Indian Princess" programs and Camp Fire Girls. Then there are the hobbyists. I didn't know about these people until a few years ago, and was surprised to find out that there are adult men and women spending their summers and weekends dressing up and playing Indian. You see them on the pow wow circuit, along with the Indian-lovers, anthropology students and "wannabes." We are supposed to be happy about all of this; flattered, in fact. We are supposed to be grateful when white people come up to us and say they are "into" Indians. We are supposed to receive with delight and surprise their desire to share our spiritual and cultural traditions, particularly so, if they say they want to "help" us. They are very offended at any lack of enthusiasm on our part, and say we are being "exclusionist." I have to say that I don't really understand this. I *do* know that these people are not interested in some human beings who happen to be called Indians. Those very traditions that a lot of people spent many years trying to beat, educate, and—from time to time—kill out of us as sub-human and barbaric, have now become a great romantic myth that they refer to as "our" Indian heritage. They will save the myth, as anthropologists are "saving" the things that were stolen from us in their museums. And the actual, human, Indian?

The truth is, we are still fighting for our lives, quite literally, both as individuals and as Peoples. There is no end to white greed. If an Indian has it, some white will want it; it doesn't matter what "it" is. From Cape Cod to Oka, from Big Mountain to the Northwest coast, this is true. Unfortunately for Native people, much of the desolate, barren land onto which so many were forced has turned out to be over some of the richest mineral deposits in the world. Ninety percent of all the uranium in the U.S.A. is on Indian land, 30 percent of the petroleum, 30 percent of the coal.[19] The Northern Cheyenne are sitting on the largest remaining deposit of high-grade, low-sulphur coal in America. Extensive strip-mining has devastated Navajo lands, and the much-publicized conflict between Hopis and Navajos over the Big Mountain joint land-use area is just a government-energy company blind for their intent to possess the wealth underlying that land. During the "energy crisis," a National Academy of Science study concluded that reclamation of strip-mined areas in the Southwest would be "virtually impossible due to the low level of rainfall received there annually."[20] The government began referring to the Navajo reservation as a "national sacrifice area." It wasn't until they began using the same phrase about the Plains states that white ranchers began to see it might be in their best interests to join the Northern Cheyenne in trying to fight off the energy companies. On Pine Ridge, one of the poorest and largest reservations, 90 percent of the available grazing land is leased to white ranchers.

During the 1970s, the government came up with Operation Bootstrap, which was supposed to help Indians help themselves. A plant or factory would be built on a reservation and leased at a very low fee to an outside corporation with the government providing workers—Indians—and trainee programs. Indians worked in the factories at half the minimum wage. When the training was completed employees were fired and owners started over with a fresh lot. In one instance, when the American Indian Movement protested these abuses on Navajo land, the company, Fairchild Electronics, simply pulled up stakes and moved the whole plant to Korea.[21]

Unemployment on reservations has always been high; now, in economic downtimes, it can run as high as 90 percent. What federal programs there were for

Native people are long gone. Health facilities are few, and the care offered in them is poor. They can be dangerous places for Indians.

In 1977, a conference on "Discrimination Against Indigenous Populations in the Americas" reported that 24 percent of Native women in the United States had been sterilized. Of 132 sterilizations performed in Claremore, Oklahoma, in 1973, only 32 were for therapeutic reasons. In Oklahoma City, 1,761 sterilizations were performed; in the Aberdeen area, 740; in Phoenix, Arizona, 784 were done within a 46-month period.[22] A General Accounting Office study reported that, between 1973 and 1976, in four Indian Health Service areas, 3,406 sterilizations were performed on Native women. Some of these women were as young as 13.[23] This is genocide—by anyone's standards, I should think.

They are still taking our children. Native children are still put up for adoption, even though laws have been passed specifying that they must be released by their Nations before they can be adopted out. As with everything, there are ways around the system. I see Indian kids all the time in the wealthy suburb of Boston where I work. Their adoptive parents say, if they'll talk to me at all, "Oh, she's from Guatemala" or "He's from South America." Children are removed from their homes by child-welfare officials whose only criteria for adequate parenting are material. Children living with relatives other than parents are particularly at risk, since the social workers have no understanding of the importance of the extended family to the child's well-being. Because of poverty on reservations both parents may have to work out. It is not that uncommon for them to come home and find their children gone. Some of these children are never found.

Average life-expectancy on reservations is still less than 50 years. Infant mortality among Native people is four times higher than the national average. The suicide rate for Indian teenagers is the highest in the world among their age-group and the leading cause of death among them. Michael Dorris, in his book, *The Broken Cord*, reports estimates of Fetal Alcohol Syndrome in 25 to 50 percent of Indian births.[24] Most Indian teenagers drop out of school before high school graduation; of those who do go to college, the drop-out rate is better (or worse) than 90 percent.

What is going on here?

In 1933, Chief Luther Standing Bear's autobiography, *Land of the Spotted Eagle*, was published in Boston. In it he said, "The white man does not understand the Indian for the reason that he does not understand America. He is too far removed from its formative processes. The roots of the tree of his life have not yet grasped the rock and soil. The white man is still troubled with primitive fears; he still has in his consciousness the perils of this frontier continent, some of its fastnesses not yet having yielded to his questing footsteps . . . . He shudders still with the memory of the loss of his forefathers upon its scorching deserts and forbidding mountain-tops. The man from Europe is still a foreigner and an alien. *And he still hates the man who questioned his path across the continent.*"[25]

At any given time, it can be physically dangerous to be Indian anywhere in this country; but out-and-out, unashamed hatred directed against Native people is only socially acceptable, now, in the places where there are lots of Indians. Bumper stickers saying, "Save a deer, shoot an Indian," tend to come from areas around reservations. But it is not necessary to shoot people in order to get rid of them. Another way, just as effective, is to make sure that they have nothing for their lives and no hope for the future—then sit back and wait. In *Man's Rise to Civilization: The Cultural Ascent of the Indians of North America* (a book I do not particularly recommend), Peter Farb had this to say: "Millions of dollars have been spent in excavating and transporting to museums the tools, weapons, and other artifacts of Indians long dead—but scarcely a penny to allow the ways of their living descendants to survive. Modern Americans are quick to prevent cruelty to animals, and sometimes even to humans, but no counterpart of the Humane Society or the Sierra Club exists for the prevention of cruelty to entire cultures."[26]

It is easy for Americans to be against apartheid in South Africa; it is thousands of miles away. When Nelson Mandela was let out of jail, you threw a nation-wide party. Who has even heard of Leonard Peltier? —political prisoner for 15 years, America's Mandela. Richard Oakes? —Mohawk—leader at Alcatraz, later helped Pit River people. Shot on September 21, 1972, age 31, by a white man known to "have strong feelings against Indians."[27] That man was charged with "involuntary" manslaughter. Pedro Bissonette? —Oglala Lakota, leader at Wounded Knee. Shot and killed on October 17, age 33, by a BIA police officer. Annie Mae Aquash? —Micmac, helped establish the Boston Indian Council, was at Wounded Knee. On February 24, 1976, her body was found on Pine Ridge. She was 31. The coroner for the BIA said she died of exposure. Her hands were cut off by the F.B.I. agents—who had been on the reservation since 1973 and knew her well—and sent to Washington for identification. When friends and relatives demanded an independent autopsy, and finally got authorization to have her body exhumed, a bullet was found in the back of her head. No one has ever been charged with her murder.

And more. And more. And more. And more.

At the end of his book, *Columbus, His Enterprise*, Hans Koning says that we will perhaps come to recognize Columbus not only as a man of his time but of his race. "And the West has ravaged the world for 500 years, under the flag of a master-slave theory which in our finest hour of hypocrisy was called 'the white man's burden' . . . . I am not ignoring the cruelties of other races. What sets the West apart is its persistence, its capacity to stop at nothing. No other race or religion, or non-religion, ever quite matched the Christian West in that respect."[28]

Nearly 200 species of birds and animals have been completely wiped out since the Europeans arrived in America, not because they deliberately set out to make them extinct—in most cases—but simply because this life served no useful purpose in their sight. One of the justifications offered for what was done to us, although with less and less credibility (I wonder now if anyone ever really believed it) is that we weren't "using" the land.

New Age people tend to be "into" Indians. One person they like to quote is the Duwamish chief, Sealth. If they can, so, too, can I.

> Your time of decay may be distant—but it will surely come, for even the white man whose God walked and talked with him as friend with friend, cannot be exempt from the common destiny. We may be brothers after all. We will see.

> Every part of this soil is sacred in the estimation of my people. Every hillside, every valley, every plain and grove, has been hallowed by some sad or happy event in days long vanished . . . . The dust upon which you now stand responds more lovingly to their footsteps than to yours, because it is rich with the dust of our ancestors, and our bare feet are conscious of the sympathetic touch . . . even the little children who have lived here and rejoiced here for a brief season, still love these sombre solitudes, and at eventide they grow shadowy of returning spirits. And when the last Red Man shall have perished, [and] the memory of my tribe shall have become a myth among the white men, these shores will swarm with the invisible dead of my tribe, and when your children's children think themselves alone in the field, the store, the shop, upon the highway, or in the silence of the pathless woods, they will not be alone . . . . At night when the streets of your cities and villages are silent and you think them deserted, they will throng with the returning hosts that once filled them and still love this beautiful land. The white man will never be alone. Let him be just and deal kindly with my people, for the dead are not powerless. Dead—I say? There is no death. Only a change of worlds.[29]

Notes:

1. *Miami News,* quoted in Barreiro, *View from the Shore,* 9.
2. Koning, *Columbus,* 52.
3. Ibid., 71.
4. Ibid., 71.
5. Ibid., 64.
6. Ibid., 64.
7. Ibid., 84.
8. Ibid., 122.
9. Ibid., 122.
10. C.I.B.C., *Chronicles of American Indian Protest,* 7.
11. Ibid., 55.
12. Ibid., 63.
13. Ibid., 112.
14. Ibid., 152.
15. Ibid., 191.
16. Ibid., 208.
17. Farb, *Man's Rise to Civilization,* 237.
18. *SubjectGuide to Books in Print, 1990-91,* 2: 3620-3665.
19. C.I.B.C., *Chronicles of American Indian Protest,* 353.
20. Ibid., 359.
21. Ibid., 355.
22. Ibid., 364.
23. Ibid., 365.
24. Dorris, *Broken Cord.*
25. C.I.B.C., *Chronicles of American Indian Protest,* 270.
26. Farb, *Man's Rise to Civilization,* 275.
27. C.I.B.C., *Chronicles of American Indian Protest,* 317.
28. Koning, *Columbus,* 121.
29. C.I.B.C., *Chronicles of American Indian Protest,* 168.

Works Cited:

Akwesasne Notes. Mohawk Nation, (Via Rooseveltown, NY, P.O. Box 196, 13683-0196.)

Ashabranner, Brent. *Morning Star, Black Sun: The Northern Cheyenne Indians and America's Energy Crisis.* New York: Dodd, Mead, 1982.

Awiakta. *Rising Fawn and the Fire Mystery.* [Memphis]: St. Luke's Press, 1983.

Barreiro, José, ed. *The View from the Shore*. Ithaca, NY: Northeast Indian Quarterly (Cornell University), Fall, 1990.

Brand, Johanna. *The Life and Death of Anna Mae Aquash*. Toronto: Lorimer, 1978.

Bruchac, Joseph. *Translator's Son*. Merrick, NY: Cross-Cultural Communications, 1981.

Costo, Jeannette Henry, and Rupert Costo. *The Missions of California: A Legacy of Genocide*. San Francisco: Indian Historian Press, 1987.

Council on Interracial Books for Children. *Chronicles of American Indian Protest*. New York (1841 Broadway, New York, NY 10023): C.I.B.C., 1979.

Deloria, Vine. *Custer Died for Your Sins*. New York: Macmillan, 1969.

Dorris, Michael. *The Broken Cord*. New York: Harper & Row, 1989.

Durham, Jimmie. *Columbus Day: Poems, Drawings and Stories about American Indian Life and Death in the Nineteen Seventies*. Minneapolis (Box 7232, Minneapolis, MN, 55407): West End Press, 1983.

Farb, Peter. *Man's Rise to Civilization: The Cultural Ascent of the Indians of North America*. New York: Dutton, 1978.

Geronimo. *Geronimo's Story of His Life*. Williamstown, Mass.: Corner House Publications, 1980, (c1906).

Haegert, Dorothy. *Children of the First People*. Tillacum Library (100-1062 Homer St., Vancouver, B.C. V6 B2W9), Arsenal Pulp Press Book Publisher.

Koning, Hans. *Columbus, His Enterprise*. New York: Monthly Review Press, 1976.

Matthiessen, Peter. *In the Spirit of Crazy Horse*. New York: Viking, 1983.

———. *Indian Country*. New York: Viking, 1984.

Nabakov, Peter, ed. *Native American Testimony; An Anthology of Indian and White Relations: First Encounter to Dispossesion*. New York: Crowell, 1978.

New Mexico People and Energy Collective. *Red Ribbons for Emma*. Stanford, CA (P.O. Box 3016, Stanford, CA, 94305): New Seed Press, 1981.

Standing Bear, Luther. *Land of the Spotted Eagle*. Lincoln: University of Nebraska Press, 1978, c1933.

Steltzer, Ulli. *A Haida Potlach*. Seattle: University of Washington Press, 1984.

Turtle Quarterly. Native American Center for Living Arts, (25 Rainbow Mall, Niagara Falls, NY, 14303) (Winter, 1990).

Voices from Wounded Knee, 1973, in the Words of the Participants. Rooseveltown, NY: Akwesasne, 1974.

Cultural Substance:
A Writer's Gift to Readers

Walter Dean Myers

We normally think of memory as the process of bringing to the consciousness those things that we've either learned or experienced. But we have memories that are part of us, that we act upon, but that we seldom bring to our conscious mind. For a long time I thought that my earliest experience of self, of being me, was a reading experience. I remember being in Harlem and my mother working with me, teaching me to read. My foster parents weren't educated people. My mother often did Day's work, that is, working by the day for people who needed their houses cleaned.

When she wasn't working my mother would sit with me in the afternoons and read romance magazines to me. I still remember sitting in that sunny room. I was only allowed on the chair that didn't have doilies on it because I used to push my fingers through the doilies when I got excited. I wouldn't always understand what she was reading. I couldn't, for example, quite get the drift of heaving bosoms.

Those moments with my mother were so pleasant, so deeply ingrained in my memory, that I often thought of them as the beginning of my consciousness. But recently I attended a conference in which a speaker, Shirley Brice Heath, talked about the childhood experience of creating a world with the mind. The moment, the very moment, I began to think about this idea, I began to remember earlier experiences in my life. She had pushed back my experience of being me to an earlier time.

I lived in New York with my two sisters (my good sister and my bad sister), my foster parents and occasionally the father of my foster father. I didn't much like this old man. Especially I didn't like his scary stories. He told endless stories about the

Walter Dean Myers won first prize in a 1968 Council on Interracial Books for Children contest with his manuscript for the picture book, Where Does the Day Go? *Since then, Mr. Myers has published 22 novels, seven picture books and three works of nonfiction. Many of his books have been selected as Best Books for Young Adults or Notable Children's Books by the American Library Association. Three have won the Coretta Scott King Award for writing and one was a Newbery Honor Book. Walter Dean Myers currently works as a professional writer and lives with his family in Jersey City, New Jersey.*

Garden of Eden, about Adam and Eve (I don't think he ever read the New Testament), and about the snake. Whatever I did, he had an Old Testament story for the particular occasion. The story I particularly hated was the story of Abraham and Isaac. Abraham took his son to the mountain and he had this knife with which he was going to sacrifice his son. Of course, being young, I saw myself as Isaac and I didn't even care if God showed up at the last minute, like a Saturday morning serial, to save Isaac. It was still a scary story.

If I complained about anything, I would get the entire story of Job. Sometimes I could avoid the stories but at other times I knew they were coming and there wasn't a thing I could do about it. For example, when my cousin Henrietta married an African man and the guy died, the whole family got together at my aunt's house and I knew the stories were coming. And they did. I went to my aunt's house (this is the same aunt that *Mojo and the Russians* was based on) and the stories came. Oh, there were stories about people coming back from the dead and knocking on your door in the middle of the night, or people that you could only see when you looked in the mirror. And, of course, I knew my aunt knew what she was talking about because everybody knew she was born with a veil over her face.

Right after the death of my cousin's husband, my father took me crabbing on the Hudson River. We lived on 122nd Street and went down to 125th Street to the old wooden piers. We had these crab baskets that you were supposed to let down into the water. The baskets had bait on the bottom and crabs were supposed to eat the bait. We'd pull the baskets up periodically to see if we had caught any crabs.

It was a very hot night and the entire pier was filled with people—Blacks, whites, Irish, Puerto Ricans—trying to escape the heat of the tenements. I asked my father for a dime for ice cream and he gave it to me. On the way back from the ice cream vendor I saw a man dressed in overalls, standing on the pier howling toward the heavens. People were standing around laughing at this crazy fool, and so I smiled, too. When I got back to my father he asked me what was going on and I told him. He said that you shouldn't laugh at people. Then he went back to his crabbing.

After a while there was another commotion on the pier and we looked to see what had happened. The man had jumped into the water. People looked over the side but the man quickly disappeared into the dark waters. The police came and after a while they recovered the man's lifeless body.

I knew he was coming back. I knew he would be coming back and be mad at me because I smiled at him. I went home with my father, and I tried to get this guy out of my mind. I went to bed and said a prayer. "Lord, don't let this man come and get me." I knew he was there, though. What I was afraid of was that when I pulled down the covers he would be sitting on the chair next to my bed. Maybe he wasn't there, maybe he was. In the morning, it took me a long time to get my head out from under the covers to discover that the drowned man wasn't there. Thank God!

I hoped that my father would not tell my grandfather about the drowned man. He did. Furthermore, my father and mother were leaving for the evening. Also, my good sister was leaving. I knew she was because I could smell the hair grease that she used to do her hair. That would leave me home with just my bad sister (the one that once lost me on 125th Street even though Mama had told her to keep an eye on me) and my grandfather.

I tried to stall the coming story by going to the window. I used my mother's window pillow. My mother had a special pillow she used to lean on when she looked out of the window. If you were poor you took a pillow from the bed, but if you had a few dollars you had a special window pillow. I leaned on that pillow and watched the world go by until it was time to go to bed. Did I tell you I had a bad bed?

It wasn't so much a bad bed as it was a spooky bed. It was spooky because I had this quilt on the bed that this woman named Goldy, who had died of sugar diabetes, had given my mother. I had avoided my grandfather's stories, at least for that night.

I didn't like my grandfather because of his stories and sometimes I didn't like my father because of his stories. When I told my mother that I was afraid of the drowned guy coming back, my father pulled me aside and told me not to worry. The guy was probably not coming back, he said. I didn't have to worry unless I heard a certain kind of rap on the wall. And then he rapped on the wall and jumped up from his chair.

"Oh, my God, here he comes now!" he yelled as he ran down the hall.

I ran after him, screaming. My mother was furious.

I didn't like my grandfather's stories. But what my grandfather was doing, besides scaring me, was passing down the cultural substance of our lives. The idea of the Old Testament, of moral being and moral judgement, that was cultural substance. He had passed it down to my father and then to me. The fear of God, too, was part of that cultural substance.

My grandfather told stories, and that storytelling is part of the cultural substance of my life, and of my people.

The smell of the grease that my sister used to groom her hair, and the quilt that Goldy gave my mother, my father taking me crabbing—all these things set me apart from the world and join me with a people who understand and find value in the same experiences.

My name is Walter Milton Myers, but I go by the name of Walter Dean Myers. The Dean family raised me, and that family, what African-Americans call the extended family, is a special part of my heritage, a part created by my people to cope with our families being split during the long night of our captivity.

What does the writer bring to the writing experience? What should I bring as an African-American? What does the Irish-American writer bring? We should bring a history of those experiences and values that identify us, that is a part of both the individual memory of the writer and the collective memory of his cultural being.

For a recent book, *Now Is Your Time*, I traced an African-American family from Norfolk, Virginia, to colonization in Liberia, to Cape Cod. The family, once it reached Cape Cod, was isolated from other people of color. After a rather lengthy interview with a member of the family, I was ready to leave when he asked me to stay a moment longer.

"You know what many people miss in their lives?" he asked.

Of course I didn't know. He went on to tell me how my brief history of his family reminded him of one of the major uses of the family concept, the transmittal of values through culture. I knew what he meant. Long before the reading experience, before we begin to make all of those defining decisions about who we are or who we want to be, there are forces that give momentum to our lives and which influence our every action and even our ability to learn.

I believe that what I have to bring to young people is the cultural substance of my experience and to recognize that experience as a celebration of African-American life. Very often young people don't even know that they are part of a culture. I must tell them that they are.

> *The grandmother of your grandmother's grandmother*
> *Has taught you a song you think you have forgotten*
> *But I hear its sweet melody when you speak to me*
> *And its chorus in the rainbow laughter of your children*
> *You think you have forgotten the song*
> *I have forgotten the same song*
>
>
> *The grandmother of your grandmother's grandmother*
> *Once brought you to the trunk of a holy tree*
> *And gave you a strength you think you have forgotten*
> *Now that you are multiplied, fallen away even*
> *from the branches,*

But in the rich blackness of your limbs,
In your earth-loving and life-loving limbs,
There is new life rising in an old trunk,
In old roots, long forgotten
I have forgotten the same roots

The grandmother of your grandmother's grandmother
Kissed the sky a thousand times in thanks for you
Her full lips pouting skyward as yours do now
The rhythm of her glad heart blending with the
rhythms of her quick hands working
Rhythms you say you have forgotten
Even as we dance through concrete villages with
Brothers and sisters who have forgotten the same
rhythms

The grandmother of your grandmother's grandmother
Laughed when you were brought home with your
secret name
And in the light/darkness of her love
She held you against the sweet smell of her bosom
Whispering new old secrets of who you are

And though you have forgotten your grandmothers
And though you have forgotten your secrets,
They still edge your laughter and still swell
your heart in the presence of God
What a delight it is for you and me to share
These gifts we think we have forgotten[1]

That is our job, as multicultural writers and people interested in the multicultural experience, to share the gift of each culture that we think we have forgotten.

Notes:

1. Myers, Walter Dean. "The grandmother of your grandmother's grandmother."

Bibliography of Selected Books Written by Walter Dean Myers

Adventure in Granada. New York: Viking Puffin, 1985.

Ambush in the Amazon. New York: Viking Puffin, 1986.

The Black Pearl and the Ghost; Or, One Mystery after Another. Illustrated by Robert Quackenbush. New York: Viking, 1980.

Brainstorm. Photographs by Chuck Freedman. New York: Franklin Watts, 1977; Dell, 1979.

Crystal. New York: Viking, 1987.

The Dancers. Illustrated by Anne Rockwell. New York: Parents Magazine Press, 1969.

The Dragon Takes a Wife. Illustrated by Ann Grifalconi. Indianapolis: Bobbs-Merrill, 1972.

Duel in the Desert. New York: Viking Puffin, 1986.

Fallen Angels. New York: Scholastic, 1988.

Fast Sam, Cool Clyde, and Stuff. New York: Viking, 1975; Avon, 1978; Penguin, 1988.

Fly, Jimmy, Fly. Illustrated by Moneta Barnett. New York: Putnam, 1974.

The Golden Serpent. Illustrated by Alice and Martin Provensen. New York: Viking, 1980.

The Hidden Shrine. New York: Viking Puffin, 1985.

Hoops. New York: Delacorte, 1981; Dell, 1983.

It Ain't All for Nothin'. New York: Viking, 1978; Avon, 1985.

The Legend of Tarik. New York: Viking, 1981; Scholastic, 1982.

Me, Mop, and the Moondance Kid. New York: Delacorte, 1988.

Mojo and the Russians. New York: Viking, 1977; Avon, 1979.

Motown and Didi. New York: Viking, 1984.

The Mouse Rap. New York: Harper & Row, 1990.

Mr. Monkey and the Gotcha Bird. Illustrated by Leslie Morrill. New York: Delacorte, 1984.

The Nicholas Factor. New York: Viking, 1983.

Now Is Your Time! The African-American Struggle for Freedom. New York: HarperCollins, 1991.

The Outside Shot. New York: Delacorte, 1984; Dell, 1987.

Scorpions. New York: Harper, 1988.

Social Welfare. New York: Franklin Watts, 1976.

Sweet Illusions. New York: Teachers and Writers Collaborative, 1986.

Tales of a Dead King. New York: Morrow, 1983.

Where Does the Day Go? Illustrated by Leo Carty. New York: Parents Magazine Press, 1969.

Won't Know Till I Get There. New York: Viking, 1982; Penguin, 1988.

The World of Work: A Guide to Choosing a Career. Indianapolis: Bobbs-Merrill, 1975.

The Young Landlords. New York: Viking, 1979.

One Hundred and One Recommended Books by and about People of Color Published in the Early 1990s

Kathleen T. Horning and Ginny Moore Kruse

How Were the Books Selected?

A careful selection of 101 children's and young adult books with multicultural themes and topics which were published in the United States and Canada during 1990 and 1991 are listed in this annotated bibliography. The books here represent recommendations based upon our wide reading and discussion of as many 1990 and 1991 books as possible through July of 1991. Therefore, the selections do not include all of the 1991 books we call to the attention of anyone looking for multicultural literature for children from infancy through age 14; neither do they represent all of the published books with multicultural themes and topics, because we do not recommend all of them. They are, very simply, the books we recommend: high quality children's and young adult books innovative in style, accurate in visual and written content, important in theme and/or unusual in insight. The bibliography represents a considerable expansion of our brief conference presentation.

Our working definition of "multicultural" refers to people of color, especially to African-Americans, American Indians, Asian-Americans and Hispanics. We use the term "people of color" guardedly and with respect to the individuals for whom this phrase or any of the above four designations seems exclusive or inaccurate. In our descriptive annotations of individual titles, we attempt to be as culturally specific as possible, basing our judgments on first-hand experience with the books. Like everyone using this book, we continue to expand our understandings of each other and of ourselves. Errors in terminology and in expression reveal areas in which we need to continue to learn from our colleagues and friends.

Most, but not all, of the selected books are by people of color. Some of the selected books are visually inclusive rather than being topically or thematically "multicultural" in content. Of the 101 titles included in this bibliography, 55 were published in 1990, 45 in 1991, and one in 1992.

How is the Bibliography Organized?

The bibliography is organized according to five age groupings: Preschool; Ages 5-7; Ages 8-11; Age 12 and Older; All Ages.

Bibliographic citations include author/editor/compiler/reteller, complete title, publisher, year, number of pages, and the international standard book number (ISBN) for each edition known in July, 1991. Addresses are furnished for small publishers. All books are hardcover, except where noted. The term "perfect binding" describes paperback editions with pages held together with an adhesive to form a book "spine", as opposed to paperback editions with pages folded and stapled.

How Can the Books Be Located?

Anyone wanting to borrow any of these books from a public library or school library media center or academic library children's literature collection or through interlibrary loan will be able to do this with the information provided in each citation. Anyone wanting to buy one or more of these books for an agency or institution will be able to place an order with a book distributor using the citations here. Anyone wanting to buy a book for personal use or for a gift can ask a local bookstore to order the book if it is not in stock. Most libraries and bookstores have the latest edition of either *Books in Print* or *Children's Books in Print* (R. R. Bowker) in which current edition information and prices are listed. It will be helpful for a librarian or bookseller if you have the complete bibliographic citation in hand when phoning or going to a library or bookstore to arrange a reserve or an order. To acquire books from small publishers, write directly and send a check with your order. For institutional ordering, inquire which distributor(s) the small publisher uses. Enclose a self-addressed, stamped envelope with any inquiry sent directly to a small publisher.

Where Can I Find Additional Multicultural Books?

See Children's Multicultural Literature Resources (p. 175) for a listing of other resources pertaining to multicultural literature for children and young adults.

Preschool

Aardema, Verna. *Borreguita and the Coyote*. Illustrated by Petra Mathers. Alfred A. Knopf, 1991. 32 pages. (0-679-80921-X)

> Hungry Coyote thinks that Borreguita, the little lamb, would make a tasty meal but every time he meets her she manages to outsmart him, leaving him not only hungry but humiliated as well. Petra Mathers' glowing, boldly colored illustrations are ideally suited to this well-paced retelling of an amusing Mexican folktale about brain winning out over brawn.

Albert, Burton. *Where Does the Trail Lead?* Illustrated by Brian Pinkney. Simon & Schuster, 1991. 32 pages. (0-671-73409-1)

> A short, lyrical text traces the steps of an African-American boy on Summer Island as he follows a rustic trail along the beach until he reaches his family at a seaside picnic. Brian Pinkney's scratchboard illustrations are colored with aqua, green, brown, and purple oil pastels, providing the perfect ambience for the quiet story of a solitary journey.

Bang, Molly. *Yellow Ball*. Greenwillow, 1991. 24 pages. (0-688-06315-2)

> Three beach-goers interrupt a game of catch to build a sand castle on a busy sandy stretch. Two individuals are African-American, one being toddler-sized. The third person involved is a white female. Their ages and roles are as open to interpretation as the rest of the events in this stunning book bearing large ideas and few words: "Catch . . . Throw . . . Uh-oh . . ." Although the people in the book don't notice, young readers will see the big yellow ball as it is carried away on the tide and begins a long journey out to sea. Bang's dazzling full-color pastel paintings tell most of the story as they trace the progress of the ball, over dolphins and under sea gulls, beyond a bridge and through a night storm, before being washed ashore on a different beach and into the open arms of another brown-skinned child.

Barbot, Daniel. *A Bicycle for Rosaura*. Illustrated by Morella Fuenmayor. U.S. edition: Kane/Miller, 1991. 24 pages. (0-916291-34-0)

> A delightful picture book from Venezuela details the predicament of Señora Amelia when her handsome hen Rosaura asks for a bicycle for her birthday. An indulgent pet-owner, Señora Amelia searches high and low but is simply unable to find a shop that caters to athletically inclined chickens. Happily, an inventive street peddler is equal to the task of building a custom-made two-wheeler. Much of the humor of this fast-paced story comes from Morella Fuenmayor's softly colored realistic illustrations which give an air of eerie possibility to the absurd.

Bogart, Jo Ellen. *Daniel's Dog.* Illustrated by Janet Wilson. Scholastic/Hardcover, 1990. 30 pages. (0-590-43402-0)

> A young African-American boy is shown adjusting to two big changes in his family life: the birth of a baby sister and the death of his grandfather. Daniel copes by inventing an imaginary dog which he is eventually able to share with his Asian playmate Norman. In her boldly colored realistic paintings, Janet Wilson demonstrates great skill at depicting the subtly expressed emotions of preschoolers through postures as well as facial expressions.

Cousins, Lucy. *The Little Dog Laughed.* U.S. edition: E. P. Dutton, 1990. 64 pages. (0-525-44573-0)

> A freshly conceived treatment of more than 50 entries explodes many prevailing ideas communicated in conventional editions of nursery rhymes. These bold, vibrant forms and figures are far from precious, and they definitely are not lily white. The illustrations encourage waking up, and opening one's eyes literally and figuratively. The mood is carefree, the characters bear mixed racial images, and the humor throughout is delightful.

Cummings, Pat. *Clean Your Room, Harvey Moon!* Bradbury, 1991. 32 pages. (0-02-725511-5)

> The Voice of Doom that Harvey Moon hears when he's settled down to watch Saturday morning cartoons is that of his mother, reminding him to clean his room. A humorous, rhyming text lists the ordinary and the extraordinary items poor Harvey has to find a place for while the colorful, angular illustrations amusingly depict the child's archetypal problem bedroom.

Dorros, Arthur. *Abuela.* Illustrated by Elisa Kleven. E.P. Dutton, 1991. 40 pages. (0-525-44750-4)

> Rosalma and her Spanish-speaking *abuela* (grandmother) spend the day together in a city park where the two of them share an imaginary flight over the city. All of Abuela's comments and observations are made in Spanish, while either the context or Rosalma's translations into English make her statements clear for non-Spanish speakers. Elisa Kleven's vibrant, mixed-media collages add colorful whimsy to this visual and verbal delight.

Hale, Sarah Josepha. *Mary Had a Little Lamb*. Photo-illustrated by Bruce McMillan. Scholastic/Hardcover, 1990. 32 pages. (0-590-43773-9)

> A modern interpretation is given to the familiar nursery rhyme as McMillan's clearly reproduced color photographs show Mary as a contemporary rural African-American child with a live white sheep. An afterword provides a history of the rhyme, the full text of the original 1830 version and a sample lesson from an 1857 McGuffey Reader which used the rhyme to teach reading.

Hong, Lily Toy. *How the Ox Star Fell from Heaven*. Albert Whitman, 1991. 32 pages. (0-8075-3428-5)

> Long ago, the Ox Star was sent to Earth to deliver a message from the Emperor of the Heavens. He was instructed to tell the people that the Emperor promised they'd eat once every three days, but he garbled the message and instead told them that the Emperor promised they'd eat three times a day. Of course, the people would need help in order to produce enough food to feed themselves so often. Bold, stylized paintings illustrate the Chinese folktale which explains how oxen came to be beasts of burden.

Hort, Lenny. *How Many Stars in the Sky?* Illustrated by James Ransome. Tambourine, 1991. 32 pages. (0-688-10104-6)

> An African-American boy is kept awake at night by a question that nags at him: just how many stars *are* there up in the sky? Pajama-clad, he situates himself in his own backyard and sets out to count them but there are too many stars and they keep moving, besides. Finally, he and his dad get into their pickup truck and head for the country, where they can get the best view of the stars. The deep blue, green, and brown hues of James Ransome's richly textured oil paintings aptly depict a nighttime suburban neighborhood as well as city and rural scenes.

Howard, Elizabeth Fitzgerald. *Aunt Flossie's Hats (and Crab Cakes Later)*. Illustrated by James Ransome. Clarion, 1991. 32 pages. (0-395-54682-6)

> Susan and her sister Sarah love to visit their Great Aunt Flossie's house each Sunday afternoon because Aunt Flossie lives in "a house crowded full of stuff and things." The sisters are particularly intrigued with Aunt Flossie's collection of hats—she has saved every hat she has ever owned and each one reminds her of a story from her past. James Ransome's elegant oil paintings move easily from the present to the past as he illustrates Aunt Flossie's stories, as well as the context in which she is telling them. A skillful use of dialogue aptly portrays a strong intergenerational relationship in an African-American family.

Hudson, Cheryl Willis and Bernette G. Ford. *Bright Eyes, Brown Skin*. Illustrated by George Ford. Just Us Books (301 Main St. Suite 22-24, Orange, NJ 07050), 1990. 24 pages. (0-940975-10-6; Paperback with perfect binding: 0-940975-23-8)

> Appealing full-color illustrations show four distinctly individual African-American children engaged in typical preschool or daycare activities, while an upbeat rhyming text describes the four: "Bright eyes, brown skin / a heart-shaped face / a dimpled chin . . ." Intended to enhance the self-esteem of African-American children, this powerful and empowering praise song is unique.

Johnson, Angela. *Do Like Kyla*. Illustrated by James E. Ransome. Orchard Books, 1990. 32 pages. (0-531-08452-3)

> A typical winter day in the life of a young African-American girl is described in a first-person text in which her older sister Kyla is the focus. While getting dressed, braiding hair, eating breakfast, playing in the snow, and walking to the store, the narrator watches and imitates everything her older sister does. A warm, loving relationship between two sisters is depicted both in the perfectly paced text and in the eye-catching full-color oil paintings.

———. *One of Three*. Illustrated by David Soman. Orchard Books, 1991. 32 pages. (0-531-08555-4)

> The youngest of three daughters in an African-American family describes the day-to-day activities she shares with her two older sisters as "one of three." On occasions when her older sisters leave her behind, saying she's too little to come along, she feels left out and lonely, until Mama and Daddy find some things for her to do at home with them. Then she's one of three again—a different kind of three, and that's fine, too . . . ." Once again, Angela Johnson demonstrates her remarkable skill at telling a good story that's just right for preschool listeners. David Soman's watercolor paintings capture the energy and emotions of three distinctive sisters.

———. *When I Am Old with You*. Illustrated by David Soman. Orchard Books, 1990. 32 pages. (0-531-05884-0)

> A warm, tender relationship between a grandfather and his young grandson unfolds through the child's verbalized projections of all the things they'll do together when the child is as old as Grandaddy: "When I am old with you, Grandaddy, we will play cards all day underneath that old tree by the road. / We'll drink cool water from a jug and wave at all the

cars that go by." Gentle, softly colored watercolor paintings show the African-American grandfather and grandson doing today all the things they look forward to doing together in the future.

Lewis, Richard. *All of You Was Singing*. Illustrated by Ed Young. Atheneum, 1991. 32 pages. (0-689-31596-1)

> A poetic retelling of an Aztec legend recounts how music came to Earth. Ed Young's brightly hued paintings move gradually from an abstract to a concrete style, perfectly expressing the sky's voice recounting the universal creation story of order emerging from chaos.

Marzollo, Jean. *Pretend You're a Cat*. Illustrated by Jerry Pinkney. Dial, 1990. 32 pages. (0-8037-0774-6)

> "Can you hiss? / Can you scat? / Can you purr / like a cat?" Rhymed verses using patterned language pose questions to children about the various actions and noises they can make to imitate 13 familiar creatures. Full-color pencil and watercolor paintings show preschoolers from diverse racial backgrounds engaged in lively imaginative play next to boxed insets containing realistic drawings of the animals they're pretending to be. Large, clear illustrations, an appealing topic, and the inviting format make this a wonderful book for group sharing and extended activities.

Roe, Eileen. *Con Mi Hermano/With My Brother*. Illustrated by Robert Casilla. Bradbury, 1991. 32 pages. (0-02-777373-6)

> A preschool-aged Latino boy describes all the things he admires about his teenaged brother who rides a bus to school, has a paper route, and plays on a baseball team. The younger brother looks forward to a time when he'll be big enough to do all those things, too, but in the meantime he enjoys the time he and his big brother spend together wrestling, playing catch, and reading stories. The simple, patterned text, in English and Spanish, is accompanied by realistic, full-page watercolor paintings.

Serfozo, Mary. *Rain Talk*. Illustrated by Keiko Narahashi. Margaret K. McElderry Books, 1990. 24 pages. (0-689-50496-9)

> Full-color watercolor illustrations and a short onomatopoeic text express the small wonders a young African-American girl notices during a gentle rain. "On the old tin roof of the garden shed the drops all try to talk at once ... Ping Ping Ping a Ding / Ping Ping Ping Ping Ping ... and they chuckle together as they run down the drain." A peaceful, uncomplicated, idyllic, rural family snapshot.

Williams, Vera B. *"More More More," Said the Baby: 3 Love Stories*. Greenwillow, 1990. 32 pages. (0-688-09174-1)

> Affectionate names for active toddlers (Little Guy, Little Pumpkin and Little Bird); exploratory activities emphasizing basic human features (belly button, toes, and eyes); repetitive baby-focused narratives centered on three times of every toddler's day (waking up, being up, and falling asleep); three loving adults guiding and caring for the babies (presumably a daddy, a grandma, and a mama); and color triads expressing the emotionally rich short pieces, which "catch up" listeners and receivers, are all combined in exuberantly unified paintings full of encircling love. The rhythmic text is painted within the larger rhythmic paintings on 11 1/4" x 10" pages. The handsome jacket art is harmonious with the warmth and excitement within this diversely pictured world of color-filled people, words, and images.

Yen, Clara. *Why Rat Comes First: A Story of the Chinese Zodiac*. Illustrated by Hideo Yoshida. Children's Book Press (1461 Ninth Avenue, San Francisco, CA 94122), 1991. 31 pages. (0-89239-072-7)

> As a second-generation Chinese-American, the author heard many folktales about the Chinese zodiac when she was growing up, but her favorite was a story that her father made up. To satisfy his curiosity about Earth's animals, the Jade King sends his messenger down from heaven, carrying invitations to a great feast for each and every animal. But the messenger trips and the invitations scatter; as a result only twelve animals arrive as guests at the feast. After their host decides to honor them by naming a year after each of the twelve, the animals hold a contest to see which of them will come first. The amusing antics of the clever, ambitious Rat win the hearts of the contest judges — Earth's children. Yen's perfectly paced text combines with brightly colored, cartoon-like illustrations to create an appealing story for reading aloud.

Ages 5-7

Adoff, Arnold. *Hard to Be Six*. Illustrated by Cheryl Hanna. Lothrop, Lee & Shepard, 1991. 32 pages. (0-688-09013-3)

> "Hard to be six / when your sister is ten. / There are things she can do that / must wait until then: when I am / seven or eight, nine or ten. / Hard to be six until then . . ." Adoff's poems about the ups and downs of a typical six-year-old who can't wait to grow up are marvelously illustrated with full-color paintings which show the six-year-old and his sister as biracial children with a white father and an African-American mother.

————. *In for Winter, Out for Spring*. Illustrated by Jerry Pinkney. Harcourt Brace Jovanovich, 1991. 48 pages. (0-15-238637-8)

> The youngest child in a rural African-American family expresses her delight with the Earth's vivid show in the ever-changing cycle of seasons. Twenty-six poems written in a young girl's voice celebrate the beauty of nature and the security of family. Jerry Pinkney's detailed pencil, water-color, and pastel paintings perfectly complement the child's exuberant moods within the cozy circle of her family.

Brusca, María Cristina. *On the Pampas*. Henry Holt, 1991. 32 pages. (0-8050-1548-5)

> A young girl from Buenos Aires, Argentina, spends the summer on her grandmother's ranch on the *pampas*, enjoying a thrilling camaraderie with her cousin and age-mate, Susanita, who knows "everything about horses, cows, and all the other animals that live on the *pampas*." Together the two girls ride horses, go swimming, search for *nandu* eggs, and listen to the *gauchos* tell ghost stories. There are plenty of activities to fill the days of these tireless and adventuresome cousins, both of whom aspire to be *gauchos* some day themselves. This autobiographical reminiscence by Argentinian María Cristina Brusca is filled with visual and textual details about life on a South American ranch.

Bunting, Eve. *The Wall*. Illustrated by Ronald Himler. Clarion, 1990. 30 pages. (0-395-51588-2)

> "This is the wall, my grandfather's wall. On it are the names of those killed in a war, long ago." So begins a picture book rendition of the first visit of a young boy and his father to the Vietnam Veterans Memorial in Washington, D. C. The child experiences other "firsts," too: weeping adults and a wheelchair-mobile veteran. The father is quiet and moved; the boy has questions. The family name and illustrations suggest that this family is Hispanic. Four sentences on the final page tell about the Memorial. Restraint earmarks a strong evocation of the emotion people generally feel at the Memorial.

Delacre, Lulu. *Las Navidades: Popular Christmas Songs from Latin America*. English lyrics by Elena Paz. Musical arrangements by Ana-Maria Rosado. Scholastic/Hardcover, 1990. 32 pages. (0-590-43548-5)

> Thirteen songs associated with Latin American celebrations of Christmas, New Year's Eve, and Epiphany are presented in their original Spanish versions as well as English translations. Full-color illustrations and brief notes accompany each song, depicting traditional activities (most from the

author's Puerto Rican background) associated with the holidays. Musical notations are included. As in *Arroz con Leche* (Scholastic, 1989) the emphasis is on traditions of Puerto Rico.

Dorros, Arthur. *Tonight is Carnaval*. Illustrated with *arpilleras* sewn by the Club de Madres Virgen del Carmen of Lima, Peru. E.P. Dutton, 1991. 24 pages. (0-525-44641-9)

> A Peruvian child describes family and community preparations during a three-day period prior to the first night of *Carnaval*. His story is illustrated with brightly colored folk-art wall hangings (*arpilleras*), which were sewn by women in Lima, Peru. A final double-page spread entitled "How Arpilleras Are Made" includes captioned color photographs of the artists at work, adding another dimension of cultural detail to the book.

Ekoomiak, Normee. *Arctic Memories*. U.S. edition: Henry Holt, 1990. 32 pages. (0-8050-1254-0)

> Seventeen full-color reproductions of extraordinary fabric art composed of felt applique and embroidery show Inuit ice fishing, *iglu* life, blanket tossing and other games, legends and seasonal events, including an Inuit Nativity. The artist's written interpretations of specific Inuit traditions integrate his personal world view with times and events almost totally past in the James Bay area of Arctic Quebec, Canada. The parallel, bilingual Inuit-English texts are visually striking. Important background information tells about the Inuit people and language, and contemporary Inuit art and artists. Normee Ekoomiak's own words describe how permanent damage to his hearing in childhood never keeps him from hearing the language of the Earth's creatures. Ekoomiak's artistic tribute to his people combined with his expressions of natural unity result in a one-of-a-kind book offering multiple levels of information and insight.

Ellis, Veronica Freeman. *Afro-Bets First Book about Africa*. Illustrated by George Ford. Just Us Books (301 Main St., Suite 22-24, Orange, NJ 07050), 1990. 32 pages. (0-940975-12-2; Paperback with perfect binding: 0-940975-03-3)

> A Ghanaian visitor to a classroom answers questions about his continent posed by a group of curious African-American children. Mr. Amegashi's natural-sounding conversation provides a wealth of information about the long, proud history and contemporary life of Africa. His comments range over Africa's history, geography, and cultures, stressing the rich diversity of this continent. Outstanding page designs use full-color illustrations and a combination of color and black-and-white photographs, all clearly reproduced and well-placed.

Greenfield, Eloise. *Night on Neighborhood Street*. Illustrated by Jan Spivey Gilchrist. Dial, 1991. 32 pages. (0-8037-0777-0)

> Each of the 17 poems in this collection offers glimpses into the lives of African-American children on a single night in an urban neighborhood. There's Nerissa telling her parents bedtime jokes, Tonya hosting a sleepover, Darnell afraid of nighttime noises, independent Lawanda determined not to let her daddy carry her from the car to the front door even though she's very sleepy, Juma talking his daddy into letting him stay up just a little longer, and Buddy, already asleep and dreaming of impressing the world with his wonderful, amazing self. Jan Spivey Gilchrist's full-color gouache paintings evoke a perfect nighttime mood in Greenfield's celebratory tribute to African-American families and communities.

Hedlund, Irene. *Mighty Mountain and the Three Strong Women*. Translated from the Danish. English version by Judith Elkin. U.S. edition: Volcano Press/Kazan Books (P.O. Box 270, Volcano, CA 95689), 1990. 28 pages. (0-912078-86-3)

> Mighty Mountain is so strong that when he walks, the earth shakes. When he hears that the emperor is holding a wrestling match to determine the strongest man in Japan, Mighty Mountain heads for the capital, certain that he can win the match easily. His confidence is eroded, however, after a chance meeting with a family of three women, all of whom are much stronger than he is. Happily, Grandma agrees to undertake Mighty Mountain's training to build up his strength for the match. A wry Japanese folktale is retold with understated humor and appropriately illustrated with amusing full-color paintings, filled with exuberance.

Hewett, Joan. *Laura Loves Horses*. Photographs by Richard Hewett. Clarion, 1990. 40 pages. (0-89919-844-9)

> Eight-year-old Laura Santana grew up surrounded by the activities at the southern California boarding and riding stable where her father is employed and near which the family lives. Riding lessons to prepare this Mexican-American child to compete in her first horse show are now added to her long-time pleasure in riding Sugar Baby bareback down to the creek. Thirty-five full-color photographs well placed on the pages picture Laura enjoying both kinds of riding, while the short text in a large typeface echoes this spirit.

Hughes, Shirley. *The Snow Lady.* (A Tale of Trotter Street) U.S. edition: Lothrop, Lee & Shepard, 1990. 24 pages. (0-688-09874-6)

> Until Mum returns each day, Samantha spends the time after school with their next door neighbor, Mrs. Dean. Sam's dog Micawber is definitely not welcome in or near Mrs. Dean's clean, orderly home and neither are any other lively Trotter Street children or their pets. One afternoon before Christmas, Sam and her friend Barney create a snow lady and name it "Mrs. Mean." Sam later realizes that the labeled snow figure is hurtful and makes a valiant effort to keep Mrs. Dean from seeing it. The racially and culturally diverse neighborhood community of *Angel Mae* (Lothrop, 1989), *Big Concrete Lorry* (Lothrop, 1990) and *Wheels* (Lothrop, 1991) is the locale for the small, ordinary incident from which Sam grows in a big way.

Keeshig-Tobias, Lenore. *Bird Talk/Bineshiinh Dibaajmowin.* Illustrated by Polly Keeshig-Tobias. Sister Vision/Black Women and Women of Colour Press (P.O. Box 217, Station E, Toronto, Ontario M6H 4E2, Canada), 1991. 32 pages. (0-920813-89-5)

> When Momma and her two daughters move from an Ojibway reservation to a city, young Polly has a bad day at school when her classmates play cowboys and Indians and tease her about being an Indian. Momma manages to soothe Polly's hurt feelings and restore her sense of pride by reminding her of some of the things their grandparents taught them about their heritage. Told in first-person from the point of view of Polly's older sister, the bilingual (Ojibway/English) text is accompanied by simple black-and-white line drawings. The straight-forward, poignant story is based on a childhood experience of the young illustrator.

Mathis, Sharon Bell. *Red Dog/Blue Fly: Football Poems.* Illustrated by Jan Spivey Gilchrist. Viking, 1991. 32 pages. (0-670-83623-0)

> The first-person voice of these 13 poems is a 70-pound quarterback who describes the ups and downs of a championship season. Some of the ecstasies of this youthful player are a touchdown, a playoff pizza, a coach's compliment, and of course, winning the trophy. And some of the agonies are trying to keep the signals straight at practice, playing a game against his cousin's team, and catching a glimpse at the face of a player on the losing team: "His face / grab something / from / my win . . . ." The action-packed, full-color illustrations show all team members, coaches, and cheerleaders as African-American.

Mollel, Tololwa M. *The Orphan Boy.* Illustrated by Paul Morin. Clarion, 1991.
32 pages. (0-89919-985-2)

> One night as an old man gazes at the sky, he notices that one of the stars is missing. His attention is soon diverted, however, when he is startled by Kileken, a young boy who seems to appear out of nowhere. After he offers Kileken a place to stay, the old man is amazed by the work the boy manages to accomplish, and he begins to question where the boy came from. His curiosity turns out to be a fatal flaw. This hauntingly beautiful, traditional Maasai story, retold by an Arusha Maasai writer who grew up in Tanzania, is accompanied by breath-taking, textured oil paintings.

Porter, A.P. *Kwanzaa.* Illustrated by Janice Lee Porter. Carolrhoda, 1991. 56 pages.
(0-87614-668-X)

> An easy reader briefly traces the origin of the African-American holiday created by Maulana Karenga in 1966 and then describes how it is observed by families today. Special attention is given to the historical significance of each of Kwanzaa's seven principles and to the meanings and uses of Kwanzaa symbols. Full-color illustrations appear on each double-page spread, adding appeal and accessibility to the text. A glossary of the Kiswahili words used throughout the book provides English definitions and a pronunciation guide.

Ringgold, Faith. *Tar Beach.* Crown, 1991. 32 pages. (0-517-58030-6)

> In one of the most visually exciting books to appear in a long time, artist Faith Ringgold has created a picture book based on her story quilt, "Tar Beach." Eight-year-old Cassie Lightfoot and her baby brother, Be Be, lie stretched out on a mattress on the rooftop of their Harlem apartment while her parents play cards with their next-door neighbors. During that magical time that comes between wakefulness and sleep, the adult conversation blends into Cassie's daydream as she envisions herself flying high above the city, claiming that she owns it all and can change anything to make life come out the way she wants it to be. Ringgold's boldly imaginative acrylic paintings brilliantly capture the power of a child's soaring imagination on the twilight edge of dreams. Set in 1939, *Tar Beach* succeeds as an appealing story for children illustrated with fine art, an astute societal commentary, and a new variation on a traditional African-American liberation motif.

Say, Allen. *El Chino.* Houghton Mifflin, 1990. 32 pages. (0-395-52023-1)

> As a child, Billy Wong dreamt of a career as a professional basketball player, but his small physical stature kept him from realizing his dream as he approached adulthood. Still interested in pursuing athletics, he

discovered on a trip to Spain that he was just the right size for bullfighting and, after years of training, achieved fame and fortune as "El Chino," Spain's first Chinese-American matador. Allen Say's full-page watercolor paintings are reproduced in black and white and full color, giving readers the impression that they are looking at photographs in a family album.

Stamm, Claus. *Three Strong Women: A Tall Tale from Japan*. Illustrated by Jean and Mou-sien Teng. Viking, 1990. 32 pages. (0-670-83323-1)

> Although the tale itself is described in the Hedlund annotation, it is important to note how this edition differs from Hedlund's retelling and also from an earlier Stamm version published by Viking in 1962. Bright colors, visual whimsy, and attention to cultural details earmark this new edition of the popular Stamm text in which the main character is named "Forever-Mountain." Claus Stamm first heard this age-old tale in Japan where it has long remained a favorite and where he continues to live.

Waters, Kate and Madeline Slovenz-Low. *Lion Dancer: Ernie Wan's Chinese New Year*. Illustrated by Martha Cooper. Scholastic/Hardcover, 1990. 32 pages. (0-590-43046-7)

> Clear photographs illustrate a short full-color photo-essay focusing on two days in the life of a young Chinese-American boy living in New York City. Readers see Ernie Wan preparing for his role as a lion dancer in a New Year's celebration in Chinatown. Family and community celebrations of the Chinese New Year are detailed.

Winter, Jonah. *Diego*. Translated from the English by Amy Prince. Illustrated by Jeanette Winter. Alfred A. Knopf, 1991. 40 pages. (0-679-81987-8)

> A poetic, easy-to-read account of the childhood and early adulthood of Mexican muralist Diego Rivera is presented in English and Spanish. Rivera is characterized as a visionary and dreamer who liked to draw the colors, people, and events he witnessed in his native land. The brief text of the 9 1/4" x 7 1/4" volume is accompanied throughout by bordered 3" x 3 1/2" exquisitely stylized paintings which dramatically lead up to a wordless double-page spread of Rivera at work on a mural, effectively communicating the magnitude of Rivera's art form.

Ages 8-11

Carlson, Lori M. and Cynthia L. Ventura, editors. *Where Angels Glide at Dawn: New Stories from Latin America*. Illustrated by José Ortega. Introduction by Isabel Allende. J. B. Lippincott, 1990. 114 pages. (0-397-32424-3)

> A brief introduction by writer Isabel Allende interprets the 500-year historical roots of Central and South American narrative. She writes of fantastic tales told before television, before radio, before writing itself. She tells of ". . . voices from . . . magical Latin American lands characterized by their wild geography, violent history, beautiful myths, legends, and people moved by their great passions." In this reference, Allende also describes the wide range of the ten brief works of fiction translated by the editors for this unparalleled collection. The writers represented are Chileans Marjorie Agosín and Ariel Dorfman; Cuban Reinaldo Arenas; El Salvadorian Mario Bencastro; Argentinian Julio Cortázar; Peruvian María Rosa Fort; Mexican Jorge Ibargüengoitia; Panamanian Enrique Jarmillo Levi; Puerto Rican Alfredo Villanueva-Collado; and North American Barbara Mujica. Differing styles and voices make each story a new adventure for readers of this handsomely designed anthology of brief works. Biographical paragraphs about the authors conclude the volume.

Chang, Margaret and Raymond. *In the Eye of War*. Margaret K. McElderry Books, 1990. 198 pages. (0-689-50503-5)

> Excellent characterizations, strong narrative dialogue, and believable relationships earmark a novel centered upon the daring adventures and growing resentments of 10-year-old Shao-Shao toward his father, who is part of the underground movement against the Japanese. Set in Shanghai during the final year of World War II, the story recreates some of the domestic and daily intrigue within the seemingly calm center of war's hurricane.

Dragonwagon, Crescent. *Home Place*. Illustrated by Jerry Pinkney. Macmillan, 1990. 32 pages. (0-02-733190-3)

> "Every year, / These daffodils come up. / There is no house near them / . . . But once, / someone lived here. / How can you tell? / Look. A chimney, made of stone / . . . Look. / Push aside these weeds — here's / a stone foundation, laid on earth . . ." Three white people — a man, woman, and school-aged girl — discover more: "A round blue glass marble, a nail, / a horseshoe and a piece / of plate. A small yellow bottle. A china doll's arm." Contemporary hikers and readers alike imagine the family which once lived here. The illustrations depict an African-American family; fragments of their conversations are imagined. Beautifully rendered full-color

paintings picture flowers and people of today, along with the imaginative flowering of life and living in another time. A reflective, quiet suggestion of others who once, too, used the same piece of earth.

Feelings, Tom. *Tommy Traveler in the World of Black History.* Black Butterfly/Writers & Readers (625 Broadway, Suite 903, New York, NY 10012), 1991. 42 pages. (0-86316-202-9)

> Significant historical events in the lives of Phoebe Fraunces, Emmet Till, Aesop, Frederick Douglass, Crispus Attucks, and Joe Louis are dramatized in a comic-strip format. Each event is introduced by Tommy Traveler, an African-American child fascinated with the private library collection of his neighbor, Dr. Gray, who has had a life-long interest in collecting books, magazines, and newspaper clippings related to Black history. As Tommy reads, he is transported back in time and becomes a first-hand observer and participant in the events he describes. Originally published as a weekly comic strip in 1958-59, this presentation of Black history is as fresh and original today as it was 20 years ago, and will appeal to a new generation of children.

Gordon, Sheila. *The Middle of Somewhere: A Story of South Africa.* Orchard Books, 1990. 154 pages. (0-531-05908-1)

> Rebecca and her family know their village is soon scheduled by the South African planning department to be flattened to make way for a new white suburban development. They become part of the movement during the mid-to-late twentieth century to oppose this forced relocation. A Black family's resistance to apartheid's injustice is seen through the eyes of a girl young enough to play with the second-hand white doll given to her mother in domestic service and—at the same time—old enough to comprehend the gravity of daily threats to her community and its people.

Hamanaka, Sheila. *The Journey: Japanese Americans, Racism and Renewal.* Richard Jackson/Orchard Books, 1990. 40 pages. (0-531-08449-3)

> As a child in the Japanese-American generation born after the war, or a *Sansei*, Sheila Hamanaka and most other Americans—*Sansei* and non-*Sansei* alike—were unaware that 120,000 American male and female citizens and residents of all ages with up to one-sixteenth Japanese ancestry were abruptly rounded up and imprisoned in ten concentration camps early in 1942. Children's book illustrator/art director Sheila Hamanaka created a mural to tell this aspect of her people's history. Hamanaka's dramatic five-panel, 25' x 8' mural depicts the World War II internment of her *Nisei* elders. The mural forms the basis for this distinctive, distinguished, and important book which witnesses to

Hamanaka's odyssey through justifiable anger. *The Journey* provides 30 close-up glimpses of mural sections. A terse, uncompromising account of the conditions of the imprisonment accompanies the close-ups. The full mural is reproduced on a double-page spread at the end. One portion of the mural utilizes the Japanese *Bunraki* puppet tradition to show U.S. military personnel acting in the "theater of war," while a *Noh* drama pose is incorporated into the section about a challenge to the imprisonment in the U.S. Supreme Court. The 9 3/4" x 11 3/4" book begins and closes with the visual and intellectual connection of tradition (the tale of Momotaro, or Peach Boy), U.S. labor history (peach picker), and hope (a contemporary preschool-aged child offering a peach to the viewer of the artistic commentary).

Hamilton, Virginia. *Cousins*. Philomel, 1990. 125 pages. (0-399-22164-6)

A three-part narrative develops several dimensions of Cammy's intimacy with Gram Tut whom she regularly visits in the nursing home. Gram emerges from this physical containment to become central to the family's effort to release Cammy from depression following her witnessing of the accidental death of a cousin. Cammy learns to welcome life's "winters" from Gram and to ". . . take what comes. Put a focus on . . . each little thing . . . Just one thing at a time. That's how it's done. Always be ready . . ." It's clear that Gram Tut is ready; and, at the close of the brief partially surrealistic narrative, so is her granddaughter. Regardless of the swirl of sudden change, the depth of one's grief and the feeling one will certainly drown, life's possibility is always at hand amidst the complexities of event and emotion. A powerful story within the emotional and technical reach of young readers.

Hewett, Joan. *Hector Lives in the United States Now: The Story of a Mexican-American Child*. Photographs by Richard Hewett. J.B. Lippincott, 1990. 44 pages. (0-397-32278-X)

Ten-year-old Hector Almaraz has lived in Los Angeles for most of his life, having come to the U.S. with his family from Guadalajara, Mexico, at age two. This photodocumentary account traces events in Hector's life in the months preceding the 1988 deadline for application for permanent residency under the U.S. Immigration and Naturalization Services' amnesty act. Hector and his family face the difficult decision of whether to stay in Los Angeles or to follow their dream of returning to Mexico.

————. *Public Defender: Lawyer for the People*. Photographs by Richard Hewett. Lodestar, 1991. 48 pages. (0-525-67340-7)

> A photo-essay describes typical activities in the worklife of Janice Fukai, an Asian-American lawyer in Los Angeles County. Black-and-white photographs accompany the straight-forward account of an individual public defender's work with clients who have been charged with serious crimes.

Hoyt-Goldsmith, Diane. *Pueblo Storyteller*. Photographs by Lawrence Migdale. Holiday House, 1991. 32 pages. (0-8234-0864-7)

> A concise first-person text and color photographs document the day-to-day life of April Trujillo, a ten-year-old Cochiti girl who lives with her grandparents near Santa Fe, New Mexico. April is a member of a gifted family—both of her grandparents are potters and her uncle is a drum maker. She describes the step-by-step process her grandparents go through to make clay storyteller sculptures, from going out to dig up the clay they will use, to kneading and shaping it and sculpting the figure, to sanding, polishing and painting it before firing it in a kiln. A deep respect for elders and cultural traditions is apparent in April's young voice, as she places every-day activities in a cultural context.

————. *Totem Pole*. Photographs by Lawrence Migdale. Holiday House, 1990. 32 pages. (0-8234-0809-4)

> David is a Tsimshian boy whose pride in his father's artistry as a wood-carver and creator of a newly commissioned totem pole provides the focus for a 10" x 10" first-person narrative. The history and culture of David's paternal elders, the Eagle Clan from Metlakatla on Alaska's Annette Island, are described and shown in full-color photographs, as is a brief background of the Klallam Indians of the Northwest Coast. Written and visual explanations detail the steps David's father takes to find a straight, tall cedar tree and carve the Klallam Thunderbird, Raven, Whale, Bear, and other symbolic images into its trunk. The community's involvement in raising and celebrating the pole's placement on the Klallam Reservation is pictured. David's maternal ancestors emigrated to the U.S. from Europe generations ago. The boy's Tsimshian heritage and Eagle Clan membership are interpreted in several ways, including the one-page retelling of the "Legend of the Eagle and the Young Child." A glossary concludes this unusual and absorbing photo documentary account.

Hurwitz, Johanna. *Class President*. Illustrated by Sheila Hamanaka. William Morrow, 1990. 85 pages. (0-688-09114-8)

> Fifth-grader Julio Sanchez is intrigued by Mr. Flores, a new teacher who pronounces Julio's name accurately and pays attention to the boy's latent leadership ability. Short sentences and brief chapters move along a new story about peer relationships which were first featured in *Class Clown* (Morrow, 1987) and *Teacher's Pet* (Morrow, 1988).

Jenness, Aylette. *Families: A Celebration of Diversity, Commitment and Love*. Houghton Mifflin, 1990. 48 pages. (0-395-47038-2)

> Seventeen young people each briefly comment upon the composition of their families in a photo-essay which originated as an interactive exhibition at the Children's Museum in Boston. One strength of this unique book rests in its organizational pattern, in that no single type of family unit is presented as standard, correct, or "other." Blended, adoptive, mixed-racial, biracial, two parent, one parent, gay and lesbian, collective and extended families from diverse racial, ethnic, and economic backgrounds are pictured. Child-expressed definitions of "family" and a list of books for further reading are additional features of a distinctive book.

Joseph, Lynn. *A Wave in Her Pocket: Stories from Trinidad*. Illustrated by Brian Pinkney. Clarion, 1991. 51 pages. (0-395-54432-7)

> A collection of tales written from the perspective of a young girl in Trinidad show her and her cousins delighting in listening to her great aunt's stories from traditional folklore. Each tale is framed by family events and activities which inspire Tantie to remember a fitting story: some of them teach, some of them amuse, and some of them scare, but all of them entertain and delight listeners and readers.

Kidd, Diana. *Onion Tears*. Illustrated by Lucy Montgomery. U.S. edition: Orchard Books, 1991. 62 pages. (0-531-08470-1)

> A short first-person novel details the difficulties Nam-Huong faces in adjusting to her new neighborhood and school, as well as to another culture after leaving Vietnam to live with guardians in Australia. Numb with grief and sorrow at losing her family and home, Nam-Huong rarely speaks, and as a result, is ridiculed by neighborhood children and class-mates. The depth of loss she feels is communicated in a series of letters she writes to a canary, a duck, and a buffalo—animals she remembers from her life in Vietnam. Numerous pencil drawings accompany this sensitive story of a young girl coping with tragic loss and taking her first steps toward

emotional healing. The author's sources include narratives of adolescent girls who came to Australia from Southeast Asia during the late 1970s/ early 1980s.

Lomas Garza, Carmen. *Family Pictures/Cuadros de Familia*. Children's Book Press (1339 61st St. Emeryville, CA 94608), 1990. 32 pages. (0-89239-050-6)

Brilliantly colored oil, acrylic, and gouache paintings illustrate scenes from the Chicana artist's childhood in Kingsville, Texas. Details from traditional Hispanic family and community life abound in the naive-style illustrations and in the brief accompanying explanatory passages printed in both English and Spanish.

McLain, Gary. *The Indian Way: Learning to Communicate with Mother Earth*. Illustrated by Gary McLain and Michael Taylor. John Muir Publications (P.O. Box 613, Santa Fe, NM 87504), 1990. 103 pages. Paperback with perfect binding. (0-945465-73-4)

Two contemporary Arapaho children look forward to times when there is a full moon. On those evenings their Grandpa Iron tells them a Full Moon Story. Each of Grandpa Iron's stories teaches reverence for nature and respect for Mother Earth. The 13 stories are followed by suggestions for creative activities children can undertake to help them remember the ecological lesson inherent within each tale.

Pelz, Ruth. *Black Heroes of the Wild West*. Illustrated by Leandro Della Piana. Open Hand Publishing (P.O. Box 22048, Seattle, WA 98122), 1990. 55 pages. Paperback with perfect binding. (0-940880-26-1)

Short biographical essays highlight the lives of African-American explorers, pioneers, entrepreneurs, and cowboys who helped shape the U.S. West. Six men and three women are featured in a highly accessible volume which pulls together hard-to-find information about Estevan, Jean Baptiste Point Du Sable, George Washington Bush, James Beckwourth, Clara Brown, Biddy Mason, Mifflin Gibbs, Mary Fields, and Bill Pickett.

Price, Leontyne, reteller. *Aïda*. Illustrated by Leo and Diane Dillon. Harcourt Brace Jovanovich, 1990. 32 pages. (0-15-200405-X)

A handsome 11 1/4" x 10 1/4" volume offers an internationally respected African-American opera star's retelling of the opera narrative which, she states, has given her "great inspiration onstage and off." In a storyteller's note at the end of the book, Ms. Price cites the qualities she admires in the Ethiopian Princess who "was my best friend operatically and was a natural for me, because my skin was my costume." These qualities include Aïda's "deep devotion and love for her country and people—her nobility, strength, and courage . . ." These characteristics are expressed in the Dillons' rich colors, dramatic costumings of characters, inventive stagings of action, and multiple uses of ancient Egyptian images. The tragic enslavement central to the opera is not romanticized, although the story contains romantic elements. Traditional typography combined with the elegance of contemporary book design and production complement the Dillons' contemporary illustrative style.

Schmidt, Diane. *I Am a Jesse White Tumbler*. Albert Whitman, 1990. 40 pages. (0-8075-3444-7)

Kenyon Conner tells about being a member of the Chicago-based tumbling team since he was five. The combination of personal discipline, tumbling expertise, team cooperation, and showmanship required of all Jesse White Tumblers is clear in 34 color photographs showing the internationally respected Tumblers performing at city neighborhood events as well as in metropolitan arenas. Kenyon's directly expressed personal account also interprets his family circumstances. His upbeat awareness of the far-reaching impacts of team activity for his life and for others develops an important dimension of the absorbing 8 1/4" x 9" photodocumentary book about young African-American athletes.

Shemie, Bonnie. *Houses of Bark: Tipi, Wigwam and Longhouse*. U.S. edition: Tundra Books, 1990. 24 pages. (0-88776-246-8)

Line drawings accompany a brief text describing the three basic types of shelters built by Woodland Indians during earlier times. Pictures show both an exterior and interior view of each dwelling, while the text explains how the structures were built and why they were particularly well suited to the environment.

Soto, Gary. *Baseball in April and Other Stories*. Harcourt Brace Jovanovich, 1990. 109 pages. (0-15-205720-X)

Strong evocations of childhood and young adolescence unfold in 11 original stories concerning ordinary contemporary youth: Michael and Jesse trying out for the Little League for the third year in a row; Lupe Medrano with a "razor-sharp mind" and the will to become a champion in one sport or another; and the young teenager who feels too old to be with the family on a vacation and too uncertain of independence to enjoy being left behind. Distinctive low-key humor, well crafted opening and closing sentences, and small surprises in external dialogue and internal action earmark brief works of fiction about Mexican-American family/neighborhood/school life in a central California valley town. The universal experiences hold high appeal for male and female readers alike. The glossary defines the Spanish language words and phrases used in context throughout the book.

Stolz, Mary. *Go Fish*. Illustrated by Pat Cummings. HarperCollins, 1991. 74 pages. (0-06-025822-5)

Thomas and Grandfather share a passion for thinking about fishing, fishing, cooking fish, eating fish and playing the "Go Fish" card game. And, of course, Grandfather always has a story to tell when Thomas fishes around for a reason to stay up just a little bit longer. Both Stolz's story and Cummings' drawings depict a strong and tender intergenerational relationship in an African-American family. An easy chapter book with black-and-white illustrations on every page continues the story of eight-year-old Thomas and his grandfather who were introduced in the picture book *Storm in the Night* (Harper, 1988).

Tate, Eleanora E. *Thank You, Dr. Martin Luther King, Jr.!* Franklin Watts, 1990. 237 pages. (0-531-15151-4)

Gumbo Grove is once again the setting for a story involving Mary Elouise, an elementary school-aged girl first introduced in *The Secret of Gumbo Grove* (Watts, 1987). Mary Eloise's pride in her African-American heritage grows appreciably throughout this contemporary story concerning personal self-esteem and racial pride. A visiting African-American storyteller and Mary Elouise's grandmother represent important mentors as Mary Elouise gains new insights. As Tate first did in *Just an Overnight Guest* (Dial, 1980), she once again reliably examines sensitive, intra-racial issues directly and effectively, using lively and believable peer dialogue and motivations recognizable to readers.

Taylor, Mildred D. *Mississippi Bridge*. Illustrated by Max Ginsburg. Dial, 1990. 62 pages. (0-8037-0426-7)

From his vantage point on the front steps of the Wallace store in a small Mississippi town in the 1930s, Jeremy Simms, a ten-year-old white boy, watches as the weekly bus pulls in to load passengers and luggage. As the seats begin to fill up with white passengers, the Black passengers are ordered off the bus. Jeremy realizes there is unfairness in the situation, but he remains a silent bystander. Interracial tensions and interactions are flawlessly depicted in a gripping story which builds to a dramatic, surprising ending. This illustrated short story is a companion to Taylor's other short and longer works of fiction set in the same locale and time.

Walter, Mildred Pitts. *Mariah Keeps Cool*. Illustrated by Pat Cummings. Bradbury, 1990. 139 pages. (0-02-792295-2)

> Summer has arrived, and so has Mariah's half-sister Denise, to whom the family adjusts, but not entirely. Outside her family, the spunky protagonist of *Mariah Loves Rock* (Bradbury, 1988) focuses her high energy on The Fabulous Five, a swim team on which she is a diver. Short sentences and chapters, quickly paced action and a large typeface invite readers with many interests into a story in a new sequence of lighthearted episodes revolving around this lively, middle class African-American girl. Walter smoothly interweaves the family observance of Juneteenth into the plot and likewise skillfully pictures a contemporary blended family with strongly held cultural values lived out with youth influenced by the popular culture of the dominant society.

Wheatley, Nadia and Donna Rawlins. *My Place*. U.S. edition: Australia in Print, 1990. 48 pages. (0-7328-0010-2)

> A powerful cultural history of a fictional Australian neighborhood begins with a double-page spread in 1988. This and 20 subsequent pairs of pages are written, designed, and illustrated according to a pattern: "My name's Laura, and this is my place . . . Our house is the one with the flag on the window . . . This is a map of my place. We've got a McDonalds right on the corner. In the . . . yard, there's this big tree . . . There's a canal . . . Mum said it must have been a creek once. It's too dirty to swim in . . ." The visual chronology moves backward to 1788, ten years at a time, through 21 decades of Australian immigrations (e.g., Asian, German, Irish, English prisoners); world events (e.g., Vietnam War, World Wars, U.S. gold rush); and economic changes (e.g., land ownerships and uses, Labor movement) affecting ordinary families. Differences and effects of cultures and classes are suggested. The tree and the water represent steady points of reference and subtle change in each decade. The people indigenous to Australia claim the dramatic final section which displays a rural landscape at sunset before the time of contact with the British. The stunning climax is an artistic, intellectual, and political reiteration of the Aboriginal flag first seen in the 1988 section of this outstanding, award-winning 10 1/4" x 9 3/4" book. *My Place* invites already-intrigued readers into repeated experiences with the narrations and detailed images.

Woodson, Jacqueline. *Last Summer with Maizon*. Delacorte, 1990. 105 pages. (0-385-30045-X)

> Margaret and Maizon, inseparable 11-year-old friends, try to picture the changes to come when Maizon leaves for the private school where she expects to be the only African-American student. Margaret's dependency upon Maizon is clarified when she experiences the finality of loss after her father dies suddenly. The author's descriptive writing and her insights concerning the women within Maizon's immediate neighborhood in Brooklyn make her first-published short novel noteworthy.

Yee, Paul. *Tales from Gold Mountain: Stories of the Chinese in the New World*. Illustrated by Simon Ng. U.S. edition: Macmillan, 1990. 64 pages. (0-02-793621-X)

> Eight original stories utilize elements of the history and culture of Chinese laborers in Canada and the U.S. Some of the fictions read like tall tales; others are literary ghost stories with unusual twists. The collection as a whole is quirky in style and imaginative in appeal. A single intriguing full-color, full-page painting illustrates each tale in this incomparable book.

Zheng, Zhensun and Alice Low. *A Young Painter: The Life and Paintings of Wang Yani – China's Extraordinary Young Artist*. Photographs by Zheng Zhensun. (A Byron Preiss/New China Pictures Book) Scholastic/Hardcover, 1991. 80 pages. (0-590-44906-0)

> The artistic genius of Wang Yani was recognized when she was only three years old and, a year later, she had her first major exhibition in Shanghai. Since that time she has created over 10,000 paintings and has had exhibitions throughout Asia, Europe, and North America. At age 16 she began a successful transition from child prodigy to adult artist, who works in the *xieyi hua* (free style) school of traditional Chinese painting. An absorbing photo-essay traces the growth and development of Wang Yani as an artist and as an extraordinary young woman dealing with the pressures of world attention, fame, and high expectations. Numerous color photographs of Yani at work and at home give young readers a close-up of her life in southern China. Fine, full-color reproductions of more than 50 of her paintings created from age two and one half to age 16 show Yani's development as a gifted young artist.

Age 12 and Older

Agard, John. *Life Doesn't Frighten Me at All.* U.S. edition: Henry Holt, 1990. 96 pages. (0-8050-1237-0)

> A collection of 85 poems about "love, families, politics, injustice, growing up, having a good time" is iconoclastic and mature in mood and global in scope. Most of the approximately 75 poets represented are from United Kingdom nations, and many are people of color. Poets represented include James Berry, Nikki Giovanni, June Jordan, Audre Lorde, Zinzi Mandela, and Kazuko Shiraishi. A distinctive graphic design complements the small typeface in this 8" x 5" volume created by Guyanese poet John Agard.

Berry, James. *When I Dance.* Illustrated by Karen Barbour. U.S. edition: Harcourt Brace Jovanovich, 1991. 120 pages. (0-15-295568-2)

> "It is that when I dance / I'm costumed in a rainbow mood, / I'm okay at any angle . . ." Drawing on his experiences growing up in rural Jamaica and in British inner-city, Berry presents 59 original poems collected here for teenagers. The dreams, fears, and boundless energy of adolescents every-where are marvelously conveyed with a Caribbean cadence.

Bishop, Rudine Sims. *Presenting Walter Dean Myers.* Twayne, 1991. 123 pages. (0-8057-8214-1)

> An unparalleled literary biography examines the works of Walter Dean Myers from several perspectives: Myers the humorist; Myers the realist; Myers the storyteller; Myers the war novelist; and Myers the artist. Bishop brings a strong sense of cultural authenticity to her interpretation of Myers' work, analyzing his books in the context of African-American culture in general and of African-American literature specifically. *Presenting Walter Dean Myers* can be read for inspiration and information by Myers' adolescent readers and for literary and cultural insight by adults.

Castañeda, Omar S. *Among the Volcanoes.* Lodestar, 1991. 183 pages. (0-525-67332-6)

> In his first novel for young adults, Omar S. Castañeda draws on his own heritage as a Guatemalan-American for a story set in contemporary Guatemala. Teenager Isabel Pacay is a Tzutujil Indian living in Chuuí Chopaló, a small town entirely populated by the Tzutujil. As the eldest daughter, Isabel is expected to take on a lot of responsibility, particularly now that her mother is ill, and Isabel resents that she has had to leave school in order to care for the household. On the inside, Isabel is filled with conflict; on the outside, she is trying to make a smooth transition from childhood to adulthood in a town undergoing political and social changes which parallel Isabel's own growth.

Gordon, Ruth, selector. *Time Is the Longest Distance: An Anthology of Poems.* Charlotte Zolotow/HarperCollins, 1991. 74 pages. (0-06-022297-2; lib. binding 0-06-022424-X)

> "Sunset is always disturbing / whether theatrical or muted, / but still more disturbing / is that last desperate glow . . ." Thus begins "Afterglow" by Jorge Luis Borges, one of 61 brief poems in English offering sophisticated understandings of the life measurement called Time. A wide range of centuries, nations, and traditions are represented in the strong collection which draws its title from *The Glass Menagerie* by Tennessee Williams. Eighteen poems are multicultural according to the scope of *The Multicolored Mirror*, while the others stem from European and other sources. Four Chinese poets from the fifth through the ninth centuries and two Japanese poets from the ninth to the eleventh centuries account for 14 of the translated poems in this handsomely designed volume containing many poems from the twentieth century. Four poems are from American Indian traditions (Hopi, Pima, Zuni, Papago) .

Ho, Minfong. *Rice without Rain.* Lothrop Lee & Shepard, 1990. 236 pages. (0-688-06355-1)

> Thailand is the locale for a dramatic, suspense-filled narrative unfolding in a rural and an urban setting. Seventeen-year-old Jiuda gradually understands some of the complex factors changing her family and village during the Thai student movement in 1973-76. The author grew up in Thailand; as a young teacher living and working there she witnessed inequities of tenant farm life, dangers of political movements combatting rural poverty, and the brash courage of idealism which her protagonist experiences. A survival theme, romantic subplot, and intense political story await readers of this compelling novel.

Katz, William Loren. *Breaking the Chains: African-American Slave Resistance.* Atheneum, 1990. 208 pages. (0-689-31493-0)

> In his introduction, the author states that slavemasters "bent history, truth, and the Bible to their purposes . . . Central to the slaveholders' reasoning was the lie that Africans willingly accepted slavery and rejected rebellion." Katz counters the false information about bondage perpetuated throughout generations through school materials and mass media in a powerful account drawn mostly from testimonies and organized in four parts: Fighting Bondage on Land and Sea; Daily Toil; Perilous Struggle; and Marching to Freedom. Autobiographies of formerly enslaved men and women, newspapers, nineteenth century antislavery and abolitionist publications and hundreds of oral histories on file at the Library of

Congress and Fisk University offer testimony to slave defiance, endurance, resilience, and bravery. Over 60 captioned black-and-white half- or quarter-page-size reproductions of photographs, drawings, posters, and other visual material about the subject create part of the book's strong impact.

Lyons, Mary E. *Sorrow's Kitchen: The Life and Folklore of Zora Neale Hurston.* Charles Scribner's Sons, 1990. 144 pages. (0-684-19198-9)

From the time of her childhood in the all-Black town of Eatonville, Florida, Hurston delighted in hearing the stories of her people. She was determined in adulthood to give this oral folk literature the scholarly attention it deserved. Lyons skillfully documents Hurston's struggles to acquire an education and to have her research taken seriously by the academic establishment. Hurston's role as a creative artist within the Harlem Renaissance and her lifelong commitment to preserving the cultural heritage of African-Americans in the U.S. South and in the West Indies are also detailed. Excerpts from Hurston's own writing are frequently interspersed throughout the text and are set apart by a distinctive visual designation.

McKissack, Patricia, and Fredrick McKissack. *Taking a Stand against Racism and Racial Discrimination.* Franklin Watts, 1990. 157 pages. (0-531-10924-0)

An eight-chapter examination of racism and racial discrimination in the U.S. first approaches motivations for acting in a discriminatory way. Other subjects covered include forms of racism; race issues and the U.S. governments; past and present leaders and activists in resisting racism; and national groups organized against racial injustice. An immediately applicable chapter addresses name calling, racial slurs, derogatory jokes, and "problem attitudes." The substantial bibliography, detailed source notes, and index extend the resources of this direct, constructive book.

Moore, Yvette. *Freedom Songs.* Orchard Books, 1991. 168 pages. (0-531-05812-3)

In the spring of 1963, 14-year-old Shirl's thoughts are on the end of junior high school and the beginning of her freshman year of high school the following autumn. When her family travels south to stay with relatives over Easter break, Shirl experiences firsthand the pain of Jim Crow laws and witnesses the courageous resistance of her 19-year-old Uncle Pete, a freedom rider. Newspaper headlines about the civil rights struggles in the South take on new meaning for Shirl once she returns to Brooklyn, where she organizes her friends to put on a gospel concert to raise funds for Uncle Pete's cause. In this fine first novel by an African-American author, the power of fiction brings history to life and offers a fictional glimpse of northern Black church involvement in the U.S. Civil Rights Movement.

Myers, Walter Dean. *The Mouse Rap*. Harper & Row, 1990. 190 pages.
(0-06-024343-0)

> An action-filled urban tall tale includes upbeat 14-year-old Mouse's summer involvements in his neighborhood's dance contest, his first romance, and events leading to cops-and-robbers-type escapades. Fast-paced dialogue full of humorous slang and priceless characterizations of peer and family interactions distinguish an entertaining story offering selected snapshots of lively contemporary African-American young teens. (Ages 11-14)

———. *Now Is the Time! The African-American Struggle for Freedom*. HarperCollins, 1991. 240 pages. (0-06-024370-8; lib. binding 0-06-204371-6)

> Walter Dean Myers writes "Before you go forward, you must know where you have been." Myers' dynamic rendering of African-American history provides three distinct dimensions for such self-knowledge and progress: a general chronological summary, specific biographical accounts, and a striking patchwork of personal ancestry. Throughout his overview of events and conditions of the enslavement of the African peoples, Myers interweaves compelling human stories. "What we understand of our history is what we understand of ourselves," he says, and so he interprets the necessary creation of the African-American extended family and the prevalence of certain means of expression within African-American life. The ringing conclusion challenges readers to think of African-Americans' past and present as those of a people fully deserving of rights and equally blessed with the gifts necessary for success. "I bring as much truth as I know," writes the author. Myers' account of the Plantation Society, his biography of the chief's son, Abd al-Rahman Ibrathima, and his interpretation of the contributions of individuals such as Ida B. Wells exemplify the three-fold way this powerful 23-chapter book contributes new information, fresh insight and — ultimately — welcomes hope to all readers.

Naidoo, Beverly. *Chain of Fire*. Illustrated by Eric Velasquez. J.B. Lippincott, 1990. 245 pages. (0-397-32426-X)

> A cinematic flow of events pictures a 15-year-old teen-aged girl and her friend who became involved in a dangerous resistance to the forced removal of everyone in their village to a remote, barren "homeland." This fictional picture of mid-to-late twentieth century contemporary Black South African youth who become politicized by realities of apartheid is a sequel to *Journey to Jo'burg* (Lippincott, 1986).

Parks, Rosa, with Jim Haskins. *Rosa Parks: Mother to a Movement*. Dial, 1992.
209 pages. (0-8037-0673-1; lib. binding 0-8037-0675-8)

> In an account of her childhood and adult life, Mrs. Parks interprets the
> personal values and experiences leading her to remain seated when told to
> move to another part of a segregated bus in 1955. She corrects errors in the
> reporting of that history-making incident and of subsequent events. Young
> and adult readers alike will be stirred by the overall portrait of Mrs. Parks'
> highly principled life made famous because of her single, intentional act.
> By being "beyond reproach" in every way in 1955 and ever after, this
> African-American citizen also became a distinguished world citizen and —
> unintentionally — a symbol of non-violent resistance to unjust laws; her
> presence on a public dais invariably brings multitudes to tears and to their
> feet. By living decades before and after the Montgomery Bus Boycott
> began, Mrs. Parks witnessed an array of injustices due to racism as well as
> the legal and social changes stemming directly from the U.S. Civil Rights
> Movement. Her commentary on these injustices and changes is extremely
> effective because of her direct participation and her full recognition of both
> the guises and the immorality of racial segregation in the U.S. The book's
> low-key tone complements its subject's self-understanding without dimin-
> ishing the import of her life wisdom. Captioned black-and-white archival
> photographs illustrate this gripping, memorable autobiography.

Soto, Gary. *Fire in My Hands: A Book of Poems*. Illustrated by James M. Cardillo.
Scholastic/Hardcover, 1991. 63 pages. (0-590-45021-2)

> In his introduction to this collection of 23 poems, Gary Soto tells his readers
> that he thinks of his poems as a "working life, by which I mean that my
> poems are about commonplace, everyday things . . ." Arranged in a
> chronological order beginning with childhood and moving up through
> adolescence and young adulthood, the poems celebrate small, significant
> moments in the life of a working-class Chicano male. Each poem is intro-
> duced with a brief anecdote that places it in the context of Soto's life. In a
> four-page section at the book's end, he answers some of the questions
> young people have about poetry.

Taylor, Mildred D. *The Road to Memphis*. Dial, 1990. 240 pages. (0-8037-0340-6)

> Taylor's powerful narrative recreates the tensions and perils for African-
> American teenagers traveling by car through rural Mississippi in 1941.
> Although the trip in Stacey's new car lasts only three days and nights, the
> distance is greater than geographic, because Cassie is traveling away from
> her loving rural Mississippi family. The protagonist familiar to readers of
> *Song of the Trees* (Dial, 1975), *Roll of Thunder, Hear My Cry* (Dial, 1976), *Let*

the Circle Be Unbroken (Dial, 1981), and *The Friendship* (Dial, 1987) is now 17 years old. Cassie's personal courage is evident in all of the Logan narratives, and it serves her well during this dangerous journey. Few choices existed in 1941 for most African-American young adults; some of the options are represented in the circumstances of Cassie and her friends. However, these teenagers did have the resources of a mid-twentieth century underground railroad, an informal network of adults who could aid them in those times of no public accommodations laws or other civil rights legislations. This historically accurate and emotionally authentic novel stands on its own for anyone unfamiliar with Taylor's earlier works.

Thomas, Joyce Carol, editor. *A Gathering of Flowers: Stories about Being Young in America.* Harper & Row, 1990. 232 pages. (0-06-026174-9)

Original fiction by authors from diverse backgrounds comprises a distinctive collection of short stories. An immense range of U.S. adolescent life is exhibited according to race, region, and economic class, and in juxtaposition to each other, addressing "what it means to be ethnic and American," according to African-American compiler/writer Joyce Carol Thomas. Other writers represented in this distinctive anthology include Ana Castillo, Gerald Haslam, Jeanne Wakatsuki Houston, Maxine Hong Kingston, Kevin Kyung, Lois Lowry, Gary Soto, Gerald Vizenor, Rick Wernli, and Al Young. The fictions differ widely in themes, styles, and tones, offering a variety of satisfying challenges for male and female readers.

Turner, Glennette Tilley. *Lewis Howard Latimer.* (Pioneers in Change Series) Silver Burdett, 1991. 128 pages. (0-382-09524-3)

An absorbing, highly readable biography tells about a great thinker, scientist, and inventor who is best known for his invention of the carbon filament light bulb. Turner's many hours of painstaking primary research in unpublished materials housed in the Schomburg Collection and extensive interviews with experts (including Latimer's grandchildren) make the life and work of Lewis Howard Latimer particularly valuable. Her style makes the information easily accessible.

Ward, Glenyse. *Wandering Girl.* U.S. edition: Henry Holt, 1991. 183 pages. (0-8050-1634-1)

A rare glimpse into the life of a mid-twentieth century Australian Aboriginal woman is offered in this autobiographical account which reads like a novel. After being taken from her mother in infancy and raised in a Catholic mission, Glenyse Ward is hired out as a domestic servant to an upper-class white family when she is 15. Working for an employer who refers to her as "my dark slave," Ward successfully struggles to maintain dignity and an identity in harsh, humiliating circumstances.

Williams-Garcia, Rita. *Fast Talk on a Slow Track.* Lodestar, 1991. 183 pages. (0-525-67334-2)

> As the eldest son in a middle-class African-American family living in Brooklyn, New York, 18-year-old Denzel finds that he has a hard act to follow—his own. Since first grade, he's been a star in his family, school, church, and community and, after graduating as valedictorian of his high school class, Denzel is on his way to Princeton. Success has always come very easily to Denzel until he attends a summer orientation program for minority students and discovers that the competition in college is stiff. His fear of failure consumes his thoughts throughout the remainder of the summer, as he tries to figure out a way to break the news to his dad that he's decided not to go to college.

Yep, Laurence. *The Lost Garden.* Julian Messner, 1991. 117 pages. (0-671-74160-8)

> In this autobiographical account, Yep compares his life to a jigsaw puzzle and describes the process of growth and maturation as a search for all the pieces—some sought out intentionally, others found by serendipity but recognized at the moment of discovery as pieces of the puzzle. The extremely interesting narrative introduces the highly-regarded author's San Francisco childhood and Chinese-American heritage to readers who already know him through many novels, including *Child of the Owl* (Harper, 1975) and *Dragonwings*(Harper, 1977).

———. *The Star Fisher.* William Morrow, 1991. 150 pages. (0-688-09365-5)

> In 1927, 15 year old Joan Lee moves with her family from Ohio to a small town in West Virginia. As the only Chinese-Americans in town, the Lees face social ostracism and overt racism from townspeople who boycott the Lee family business. Joan herself feels tensions between the pressure at home to follow strict Chinese traditions and the pressure at school to assimilate into a white American mainstream. The Chinese folktale of the star fisher, a bird/woman caught between two worlds, provides the central metaphor for this rich, witty, engrossing novel.

All Ages

The Big Book for Peace. Edited by Ann Durell and Marilyn Sachs. Dutton, 1990. 120 pages. (0-525-44605-2)

> A unique family anthology offers an album of pieces by 31 contemporary children's book creators, including writers Mildred Pitts Walter and Yoshiko Uchida; reteller John Bierhorst; and artists Leo and Diane Dillon, Jerry Pinkney, and Allen Say. Walter's powerful short account concerning a nonviolent African-American civil rights demonstration in Washington, D.C., and Uchida's epistolary fictional narrative originating in a Japanese-American internment camp extend the concept of peace to embrace social justice issues. Jacket art by Maurice Sendak introduces the unparalleled compilation which bears the intent of offering alternate resolutions for various barriers to understanding and justice.

Bryan, Ashley. *All Night, All Day: A Child's First Book of African-American Spirituals.* Musical arrangements by David Manning Thomas. Atheneum, 1991. 48 pages. (0-689-31662-3)

> The words and music to 20 spirituals are accompanied by luminous full-color paintings. Ashley Bryan's art provides a lush, visual interpretation of well-known songs such as "I'm Going to Eat at the Welcome Table," "Peter, Go Ring the Bells," and the title song, "All Night, All Day." This is a welcome addition to Bryan's earlier children's books interpreting this distinctive African-American contribution to the music of the U.S.

Langstaff, John, selector and editor. *Climbing Jacob's Ladder: Heroes of the Bible in African-American Spirituals.* Illustrated by Ashley Bryan. Piano arrangements by John Andrew Ross. Margaret R. McElderry/Macmillan, 1991. 24 pages. (0-689-50494-2)

> A triumphant tone characterizes the nine spirituals from Hebrew Scriptures (Old Testament), selected for this companion volume to *What a Morning! The Christmas Story in Black Spirituals* (McElderry/Macmillan, 1987) Ashley Bryan's original tempera paintings visually illustrate and celebrate the strength of the stories about Noah, Abraham, Jacob, Moses, Joshua, David, Ezekiel, Daniel, and Jonah. Langstaff's selections and musical notations appear chronologically; a note about each personage provides important background; and a page at the end offers advice to adults and instrumentalists.

Mattox, Cheryl Warren. *Shake It to the One that You Love the Best: Play Songs and Lullabies from Black Musical Traditions.* Illustrated by Varnette P. Honeywood and Brenda Joysmith. Warren-Mattox Productions (Distributed by JTG of Nashville,

102 C 18th Avenue South, Nashville, TN 37212), 1990. 54 pages. Paperback with stapled binding. (0-9623381-0-9)

> The music and lyrics for 16 play songs and 10 lullabies from African-American culture are included in this visually and culturally rich, beautifully designed collection. Each song is bordered by a strip of Kente cloth, reproduced in full color, and accompanied by brief information about its historical and cultural context. Each play song also includes a brief description of the game or activity traditionally associated with the song. Ten full-color reproductions of paintings by gallery artists Varnette P. Honeywood and Brenda Joysmith show children at home and at play, providing a perfect complement to the spirit of the songs.

Slier, Deborah, editor. *Make a Joyful Sound: Poems for Children by African-American Poets*. Illustrated by Cornelius Van Wright and Ying-Hwa Hu. Checkerboard, 1991. 108 pages. (0-56288-000-4)

> A thick volume, generously illustrated, pulls together 75 poems from diverse sources by well-known poets (Lucille Clifton, Countee Cullen, Eloise Greenfield, Langston Hughes), as well as others who rarely appear in children's poetry anthologies (Kali Grosvenor, Nanette Mellage, Useni Eugene Perkins, Quincy Troupe). These poems for young children touch on such topics as family, friends, playing outside, and school, in addition to cultural pride and African-American heritage. The overall effect of this marvelously rich anthology is best expressed by one of the selections by Mari Evans: "Who / can be born black / and not / sing / the wonder of it / the joy / the challenge . . ."

Steele, Susanna and Morag Stiles, ed. *Mother Gave a Shout: Poems by Women and Girls*. Illustrated by Jane Ray. U.S. edition:Volcano Press (P.O. Box 270, Volcano, CA 95689), 1991. 126 pages. (0-912078-90-1)

> A lively collection of over 100 poems written by women and girls is exemplary for its multicultural perspective. Poems about identity, nature, women's work, dreaming, grandmothers, mothers, and daughters are gathered together from a wide range of traditional and contemporary sources, and feature such poets as Maya Angelou, Nikki Giovanni, Judy Grahn, Grace Nichols, Sylvia Plath, Sappho, Alice Walker, and Charlotte Zolotow. Exquisite black-and-white vignettes reinforce the multicultural focus and enhance the celebratory tone.

Commentaries on Cultural Authenticity and Accuracy in Multicultural Children's and Young Adult Books

Small group book discussion is central to all CCBC functions, and as such, opportunities for book discussion are purposefully built into CCBC conferences, workshops, and special events, in addition to being regularly scheduled each month. Attendees at the Multicolored Mirror conference participated in book discussions groups featuring the following 16 books, each selected for its relevance to the conference theme. Conference participants elected to attend book discussions in one of three categories: Preschool – Grade 2, Grades 2– 6, Grades 7– 9.

As book discussion is a group process without a formal outcome, we are unable to present summaries of the many substantial book discussions which took place at the conference. Instead, the following commentaries focusing on the cultural substance of each book were written by conference participants and local experts. The authors of the book commentaries are each from the race, culture or national origin represented in the book.

Preschool – Grade 2

Hello, Amigos! by Tricia Brown. Photographs by Fran Ortiz. Henry Holt, 1985. 48 pages. (0-8050-0090-9)

> Forty-two pages of black-and-white photographs, accompanied by a brief, first-person narrative text, follow the course of events, from morning to night, in the seventh birthday of Frankie Valdez, a Mexican-American child living in the Mission District in San Francisco. A glossary of fifteen Spanish words used in the text is included.
>
> This book is valuable for the cultural authenticity of its photographs of scenes from Frankie's everyday life and from his birthday celebration. The depth and richness of Frankie's Mexican-American culture are highlighted as we follow him from his bilingual classes in the morning to his night-time prayer before votive candles at his church. Yet *Hello, Amigos!* is seriously flawed in the cultural authenticity of its text. One frequently gets the feeling

that the first-person narrative is the result of what the author thought would be amusing for Frankie to say. Beyond its tone, however, the text also seems stilted in its use of Spanish and even contains one misspelling (the correct word is "*molcajete,*" not "*molcajate,*" for the stone mortar in which avocados are mashed). The text also fails to give such basic information about Frankie as his age and grade — one has to count the candles on his birthday cake to know he's turning seven, and it's never clearly stated whether he's in first or second grade. This failure demonstrates the unfortunate disregard of the author for the complexity of her material, both as an adult trying to sound like a child, and as a native English speaker trying to use Spanish to sound genuinely ethnic — and missing the mark.

Ana Nuncio
Needham, Massachusetts

How My Parents Learned to Eat by Ina R. Friedman. Illustrated by Allen Say. Houghton Mifflin, 1984. 32 pages. (0-395-35379-3) (pbk. 0-395-44235-4)

How My Parents Learned to Eat opens with a picture of the narrator, a young Asian girl with slanted eyes and a typical bowl-type haircut with straight bangs. What is special here is that the girl has reddish-brown hair instead of the usual jet black. In this way we know she is biracial. The child goes on to relate the story of how her parents, one Japanese and the other a Caucasian-American, met and fell in love in Japan. By focusing on the awkwardness each parent experienced with the eating utensils of the others' native land, the story presents a charming metaphor for the contrast and blending of two cultures.

As a mother of biracial children, I was immediately drawn to this book. While the story and pictures certainly held my daughter's attention, there was one aspect to the book which did not coincide with my own cultural experience as a third generation Japanese-American (*Sansei*). In my parent's house we used two kinds of chopsticks. Japanese chopsticks were called "*hashi*" and are generally lacquered with tapered ends. Japanese meals were eaten with *hashi*. It was only when we went out to Chinese restaurants that we ate with "chopsticks," usually bamboo or plastic without tapered ends and the same diameter from top to bottom.

I grew up associating the term "chopstick" with the Chinese kind. Indeed, the term chopstick is of Chinese origin. Therefore use of the term "chopstick" did not sit quite right with me. I believe the problem lies in the limits of the English language which recognizes only the generic "chopstick." I find it ironic that while the book mentions the subtle difference between the English and American manner of using a knife and fork to eat peas and mashed potatoes, the Japanese woman says "a chopstick is a chopstick." This is plainly erroneous as most people of Chinese or Japanese ancestry are aware of the differences in chopsticks. Just as sukiyaki and sushi have entered our everyday vocabulary, it might be well to continue to expand this trend and use the original native words in the text when referring to concepts where English words are inaccurate or insufficient to convey the meaning of something based in a non-English culture.

June K. Inuzuka
Denver, Colorado

Nine-in-One, Grr! Grr!: A Folktale from the Hmong People of Laos retold by Blia Xiong. Adapted by Cathy Spagnoli. Illustrated by Nancy Hom. Children's Book Press (5925 Doyle St., Suite U, Emeryville, CA 94608), 1989. 32 pages. (0-89239-048-4)

When the great god Shao grants the mother tiger's wish for nine baby tigers every year, the tiger is afraid she might forget the words the great god Shao told her she must remember to receive her cubs. Tiger makes up a song and sings all the way back to earth, "Nine-in-one, Grr! Grr!" The big black bird hears her and thinks that very soon there will be more tigers than others on the earth. The bird plans to scare the tiger so she will forget the words. Bird tells the tiger to sing the song in reverse: "One-in-nine, Grr! Grr!" That is why not many tigers live on the earth today.

When I was still small back in my homeland, I believed the tiger always had three or four babies. Then my parents told me many times about the "nine-in-one" story. I always believed there was one great god Shao living in the sky. He was the one that had power and could grant the wishes of all living things. The great god Shao could understand and talk to human beings and animals. From my point of view, both the text and illustrations are true to the Hmong art and culture. When I first took a look at the book, I recognized right away that it was from the Hmong art and storytelling tradition.

Yai Lee
Madison, Wisconsin

The Patchwork Quilt by Valerie Flournoy. Illustrations by Jerry Pinkney. Dial, 1985. 32 pages. (0-8037-0098-9)

A warm family story evolves around the completion of a quilt made from scraps of personal clothing, ragged pants, a Halloween costume, a worn out work shirt, and a new party dress. In a three-generation household, Grandma works daily on her "masterpiece," daughter is slightly upset about the "mess" the scraps seem to make, and granddaughter Tanya is fascinated with the project.

As the quilt grows, the bond between the family members grows, climaxed by complete togetherness when Grandma becomes ill and unable to do any sewing. With everyone involved the quilt becomes more than just a work of art; it seems to represent a family's history. Lest one should question how Tanya could sew so expertly so soon, it might be attributed to family tradition since Grandma had been taught to sew when she was Tanya's age.

Award-winning illustrator Jerry Pinkney captures the essence of the text and enriches the plot with carefully crafted pictures. He brings to life the middle-class family home, the daily activities, the distinctive patches in the quilt. But most notable is the artist's portrayal of the family members. He shows respect for the individual characteristics of each one—hair styles, facial contours, clothing choices, and very particularly skin tones with the message that black is every shade of brown.

The blend of text and pictures make *Patchwork Quilt* not only a satisfying story, but one that might inspire families who share the book to perhaps start a "masterpiece" of their own.

Henrietta M. Smith
Delray Beach, Florida

Where Did You Get Your Moccasins? by Bernelda Wheeler. Illustrated by Herman Bekkering. Pemmican Publications (411-504 Main St., Winnipeg, Manitoba R3B 1B8, Canada), 1986. 27 pages. (pbk. 0-919143-15-6)

In a modern-day urban classroom setting, Jody answers his classmates questions about the beaded moccasins he has brought to school that day. Answers lead to more questions, and Jody becomes the storyteller with his classmates and teacher as his participatory audience. The story is told in a circular fashion, retracing the steps of the traditional process of making moccasins, beginning and ending with the moccasins in hand.

Bernelda Wheeler is Cree. She believes that the indigenous people of this continent need to "keep in touch with each other, to portray ourselves and to educate the public . . ." (p. 27). She stays true to her goals in this story. Although Jody is never identified outright as "Indian," the essence of a Native American perspective is subtly but clearly portrayed—not only in Wheeler's writing, but also in Herman Bekkering's illustrations. Jody does not wear the moccasins to school, nor does he dress in any way that is different from the other children in his class. Jody's grandmother and father are shown as present-day people carrying on their age-old and traditional tasks in a modern-day (if rural) world. The highly detailed penciled drawings show faces that are expressive and real. The text and its illustrations work together to create an authentic image of a modern-day Native American child. Few Native American people have escaped the experience of having to answer questions about their heritage. Here, finally, is a child that young Native American readers today will be able to recognize and relate to. The message of this story is one of change and persistence—not one that presents Native people as static artifacts, nor as a dying culture. Things that change mix with things that stay the same in the dynamics of all human life. This mixture of old with new, traditional ways with modern ways is most perfectly stated in the story's ending when Jody is asked, "Where did she (grandmother) get the beads?" To which Jody replies with a mischievous grin, "From the store."

Cathy Caldwell
Madison, Wisconsin

Grades 2–6

Baseball in April and Other Stories by Gary Soto. Harcourt Brace Jovanovich, 1990. 111 pages. (0-15-205720-X)

The eleven short stories in this collection are more like vignettes than fully developed narratives in their graceful, often poetic, depiction of moments or episodes in the lives of various Mexican-American children and adolescents growing up in Fresno, California. Most often these stories deal with the desires, failures, and coming to terms with failures that their characters experience. A three-page glossary of the Spanish used in the stories is given at the end of the collection.

The stories in *Baseball in April* succeed because they are accurate, powerful evocations of the often confused and highly-charged logic, emotions, and speech of children and adolescents. Yet these stories are also a particular triumph in the subtlety and originality of the details and themes that convey their cultural authenticity. For example, there is no heavy-handed, predictable Mexicanness to these stories—no insistence on piñatas, serenades, guacamole, or prayers to the Virgin of Guadalupe. Yet in "Two Dreamers," one of the finest stories in this collection, there is a quintessential Mexicanness in the grandson's respect for his grandfather (as well as in his healthy suspicions about what he might be up to), and in the grandfather's yearning to return to Mexico a rich man, to impress "all the people" in his hometown. Soto's fine, gently humorous, almost oblique perspective on Mexican culture makes these stories a pleasure to read.

Ana Nuncio
Needham, Massachusetts

The Journey: Japanese Americans, Racism and Renewal by Sheila Hamanaka. Orchard, 1990. 40 pages. (0-531-08449-3)

The Journey originated from a mural of five panels, eight feet high and twenty-five feet long, by artist, Sheila Hamanaka. Hamanaka is said to have created the piece as a "personal inquiry" into the internment experience of her family and 120,000 other Americans of Japanese ancestry during World War II. This nonfiction book uses vivid images from the mural to relate the story of this tragic chapter in American history. It employs an attractive picture book layout and clear, cogent text to communicate the devastating impact of this experience on the Japanese-American community.

This book is an excellent historical resource for older elementary school children. There is almost nothing in terms of picture books for children on this topic. Most literature on the internment is written for juvenile and adult readers. However, I hesitate to recommend it for very young children (preschool to first or second grade) due to the dark, almost nightmarish quality of the pictures. As an adult of Japanese ancestry whose family was also interned during the war, I found the illustrations very evocative and powerful. However, it is not something I would feel comfortable reading to my young children (ages 1-5) before bedtime. I got the impression the art work was not originally created with a children's picture book in mind, rather, that someone subsequently came up with the idea of preserving the mural by creating a picture book. As such, there is a sense the book doesn't quite work for young children who might find the illustrations disturbing and the historical text dry and intimidating. Nevertheless, Hamanaka'a *Journey* remains an important contribution to children's literature and is valuable for both parents and teachers.

June K. Inuzuka
Denver, Colorado

Justin and the Best Biscuits in the World by Mildred Pitts Walter. Illustrated by Catherine Stock. Lothrop, Lee & Shepard, 1986. 122 pages. (0-688-06645-3) (pbk. 0-679-80346-7), Knopf, 1991.

In this warm family story, twelve-year-old Justin feels unfairly put upon as the only male in a household which includes his widowed mother and two older sisters. Until his grandfather helps him see things differently, Justin rebels against all chores which he perceives as "women's work."

With a writing style that appeals to young readers, Walter has developed what could have been a slight novel about cooking and cleaning into a book replete with historical information, wise advice, and an unforgettable picture of a strong Black family.

The author provides authentic information about the Black cowboys who helped to develop the West. In how many quality biographies or well-researched histories of the U.S. do readers learn of these men? Children will learn that a Black cowboy taught Theodore Roosevelt how to break horses and another taught the comedian Will Rogers how to do rope tricks. Surely some young reader's curiosity would be piqued to find out more about Deadwood Dick. Just the name conjures up adventure and daring do!

In a race of people whose genealogy is obscured in the degradation of slavery, Justin learns how his forbearers defied the threats of night riders and moved the family west from the slave-based South. The telling rings with truth. An understanding grandfather skillfully weaves historic infor-mation with the importance of such "mundane" chores as making a bed, washing dishes or learning to make prize-winning biscuits. There is a poignancy and intimacy when the grandfather assures Justin, and through Justin, other youthful males, that it is all right for a MAN to cry: "The brave hide their fears, but share their tears. Tears bathe the soul." (p. 68)

In this thoughtful novel touched with humor, young readers share in a growing experience seen from the perspective of a believable, strong Black family.

Henrietta M. Smith
Delray Beach, Florida

Kimako's Story by June Jordan. Illustrated by Kay Burford. Houghton Mifflin, 1981. 42 pages. (0-395-31604-9)

In this slice of life vignette, self-assured Kimako shares with her peers some of the activities and ideas that fill her days as an eight-year-old living in an inner-city tenement.

The relationship of love and warmth is undeniable in such small examples as how close Kimako can sit by her mother as she braids her hair in cornrows, and on a larger scale, in the explanation given as to why she must, for safety, stay in the apartment when her mother has to go to work.

The author's concern for the mind of a child can be discerned in Kimako's child-like evaluation of constant TV viewing: "It's like walking on two legs. I mean, so what?" (p. 12) and Kimako's response to a woman who wants to buy books for her: "I figure if she gives me three dimes instead, I can buy some candy of my own . . ." (p. 29). Kimako's experiments with rhyme invite participation on the part of the reader.

At first glance, the simple line drawings give the book the air of a period piece. The careful scrutiny which the intended audience is wont to give will, however, reveal interesting details that many times extend the simple text—the men in the park playing checkers, the place of the homeless man, etc.

The natural bond of affection between Kimako and the dog she is baby-sitting provides one of the few touches of humor to a book whose under-lying tone is one of serious and creative thinking, as if the author has given you a glimpse of her child self.

Henrietta M. Smith
Delray Beach, Florida

Nathaniel Talking by Eloise Greenfield. Illustrated by Jan Spivey Gilchrist. Black Butterfly/Writers & Readers Publishing (P.O. Box 461, Village Station, New York, NY 10014), 1989. 28 pages. (0-86316-200-2)

> *Nathaniel Talking* sings! This is a collection of original poems, some of which appeared earlier in the periodical, *Ebony, Jr.* The rhythmic words invite the reader to join in Nathaniel's celebration of life, his joyful future plans of "moving through the world doing good and unusual things."

> There is a refreshing naturalness in the selection of episodic pieces treating matters of concern to an irrepressible nine year old who happens to be Black. The poems speak of friendship, love, irrevocable loss, the quest for knowledge, ball games, and music.

> Gilchrist's drawings of Nathaniel and his companions are identifiably those of Black children—portrayed with care and dignity and an appreciation of their blackness.

> Going full-cycle, award-winning poet Eloise Greenfield "sings" young readers the techniques of the "twelve-bar blues" and provides a sample practice piece. Yet the child of today will find himself in Nathaniel's rap talk.

> *Nathaniel Talking* is a handsome cross-generational book of pictures and lyrical poetry that, like Nathaniel himself, "has a lot to say" to children and adults of all cultures. And it must be said out loud.

> Henrietta M. Smith
> Delray Beach, Florida

The People Shall Continue by Simon Ortiz. Illustrated by Sharol Graves. Revised edition: Children's Book Press (1461 Ninth Avenue, San Francisco, CA 94122), 1988. 24 pages. (0-89239-041-7)

> This narrative poem on American history comes from an exclusively Native American perspective. Its events are traced chronologically beginning with pre-contact origin myths, moving on through the contact years of destruction and displacement and ending with the present-day struggles of the People to regain their integrity and maintain their heritage. The philosophical perspective or world view of the narrative is expressed cyclically and ends as it began. The People remember the songs, the stories, and the concepts of interdependency and shared responsibility that all

humanity must assume in order to continue to survive into the future. The last line of this story tells us: "With that humanity and the strength which comes from our shared responsibility for this life, the People shall continue."

This book with its vision of pride and hope for the People it represents sounds both the poetic voice and the voice of empowerment that Simon Ortiz is known for. This is also a voice of enlightenment for those who wish to see with a Native eye. But for those who cannot (or will not) accept this version of American history, this voice may threaten or offend. What is most amazing about this story is its ability to say so much in so few words. It is authentic in form as well as in what it has to say. The grand simplicity of its language, the cataloging of images, and the circularity of its thought all simulate oral tradition. The illustrations complement the story's commitment to authenticity. Sharol Graves, the illustrator, accurately depicts regional and tribal differences between style of dress, physical characteristics, and diversity of art forms in her portrayals of the People. Her colors move with their vividness. As the editor, Harriet Rohmer says, "Essentially, this is a teaching story . . ." Those who feel threatened by this story's exclusively Native American perspective are not recognizing its teaching potential and risk being blinded by their own biases.

Cathy Caldwell
Stevens Point, Wisconsin

Grades 7–9

The Abduction by Mette Newth. Translated from the Norwegian by Tiina Nunnally and Steve Murray. U.S. edition: Farrar, Straus & Giroux, 1989. 248 pages. (0-374-30008-9)

This is the story of the capture, torture, and enslavement of two seventeenth century Inuit youth by Norwegian slavers. It is told from two perspectives—those of the Inuit girl, Osugo, and her Norwegian "guard," Christine.

As we focused on the book's portrayals of Inuit values and customs, we were not convinced that they are accurate. The author credits her knowledge of the culture of seventeenth century Greenland to Inuit "singers, poets, and storytellers" and their "intermediaries." She claims that because she has learned some things about Inuit culture—the people's "relationship to each other and to nature"—it is "not difficult to reconstruct their feelings as they meet the Norway of that day" (246-47). We agree that the stories of the capture, torture, and enslavement of Native people need to be told. But Ms. Newth goes beyond that responsibility and attributes thoughts, emotions, and perceptions to Osuqo and Poq. We maintain that such feelings and perceptions, rooted in the beliefs and understandings of Inuit spirituality, cannot be accurately interpreted or expressed by an author (or perhaps, in this case, translators) of another culture.

Thus we have concerns with such expressions as "unclean blood" (p. 6), "magic words and amulets" (p. 73-74), "not of our race" (p. 106), as well as with the description of the hunt for the "enchanted bear," the suicide of Osuqo's elderly grandparents, and the captives' thoughts and reflections during their trial for witchcraft, among others. The task of creatively sharing historical truth with young readers, without getting into cultural misinterpretation, is not a simple one. But we believe that Ms. Newth has stepped over the fragile line separating appropriate cross-cultural story-telling from inappropriate.

In our view, *The Abduction* is a "mixed blessing" and thus deserves a mixed review. Its bold telling of extremely painful details of history, as well as its lyrical prose and vivid descriptions, make it truly unique reading for any adult, young or old. On the other hand, its well-meaning but questionable portrayal of Inuit culture by a non-Inuit person, as well as its tendencies toward the non-credible and romantic, suggest that a warning label be placed on the cover—"Caution: May be dangerous to your multicultural health and understanding."

Dorothy L. Davids and Ruth A. Gudinas
Gresham, Wisconsin

Anthony Burns: The Defeat and Triumph of a Fugitive Slave by Virginia Hamilton. Alfred A. Knopf, 1988. 193 pages. (0-394-98185-5)

From the very juxtaposition of the words in the sub-title to a gratifying conclusion, this biography draws the reader into a tension-filled experience. After years of enduring the ignominy of slavery, young Anthony Burns escapes to Boston where he enjoys four months of relative freedom before being arrested and tried as a runaway slave.

Based on extensive research and well documented, Hamilton has recorded the series of events surrounding Burns' life as a slave, a prisoner, and finally as a freeman and minister, before his untimely death at the age of 28. The author chose to write the documentary from Burns' perspective rather than from that of the many men (and women) already well-known as activists in the abolitionist movement.

Through a deftly handled flashback technique and a melodic use of Black dialect, the imprisoned Anthony, going "inside himself," shares scenes with readers that ironically were the "happiest times." Through this device, the reader is introduced to the shames of the slave system—women designated as breeders, the dichotomous position of the Black overseer—able to mete out punishment to the slave, but subject to humiliating punishment at the hands of the master. Anthony himself, pictured as a sometimes favored child, is never totally free of physical and mental abuse. Survival came from the bond of love and support among members of the slave "families."

The purposeful suspense with which the author reports the progress of Burns' trial provides a vehicle for explaining the complexities of the existent legal system, and the conflict between state and federal law, often resulting in the questionable authority of the judge. In this setting the reader witnesses the chicanery of the pro-slavery advocates and the often thwarted abilities of the abolitionists seeking Burns' release.

Anthony Burns is a testimony to the strength of the human spirit and a source of pride and inspiration to all who love "free-dom."

Henrietta M. Smith
Delray Beach, Florida

The Education of Little Tree by Forrest Carter. Foreword by Rennard Strickland. Delacorte, 1976. 216 pages. (0-440-02319-X) University of New Mexico Press, 1990 (pbk. 0-8263-0879-1)

Little Tree is orphaned at the age of five and goes to live with his Cherokee Indian grandparents. This is the story of the years that follow. Except for the short time that Little Tree spends in an orphanage, he lives with his grandparents until their deaths, and this is where the story ends. Little Tree's story of his life with his grandparents is rich with visual imagery, cultural teachings, memorable characters, and adventures filled with both humor and danger.

In the chapter called "I Kin Ye, Bonnie Bee" Little Tree describes his grandparents in this way: "To them, love and understanding was the same thing. Granma said you couldn't love something you didn't understand." The essence of this story lies in these words. Little Tree's education is more than learning words in a dictionary or listening to Granma read from works of English literature. Being Cherokee is not presented as something that a person is simply born into. There is no "Indian Instinct" patronized here. Little Tree's Cherokee heritage is shown as a particular way of seeing and reacting to the world and as something that Little Tree must be taught. Cherokee culture is lovingly and convincingly represented in the characterizations of Little Tree's grandparents. Despite the author's tendency at times to romanticize certain aspects about them, Granma and Granpa are presented as real and very human people. Granpa's expertise and vast knowledge includes not only all there is to know about the natural world, but also all one needs to know about running a still and cussing. Granma's great capacity for kindness becomes an act of misjudgment when the moccasins that she makes for a sharecropper's daughter result in the girl being beaten. The grandparents learn from the grandchild as he learns from them, and this story becomes a rite of passage for all — including the reader.

Cathy Caldwell
Madison, Wisconsin

Fallen Angels by Walter Dean Myers. Scholastic/Hardcover, 1988. 309 pages. (0-590-40942-5) (pbk. 0-590-40943-3)

Fallen Angels is a gripping young adult novel based on the Vietnam War, seen through the eyes of seventeen-year-old Harlemite Richie Perry. Perry, a recent high school graduate, street-wise, war-innocent, is mistakenly sent to Vietnam rather than to a stateside location. The nonchalance with which Perry accepts the error: "I had heard there was going to be a truce and there wouldn't be any fighting," soon changes. He is a soldier in a fighting war! From that moment on the reader is in the war with Perry.

Through vivid yet controlled descriptions the reader witnesses the devastation of war, hears the graphic and explicit language of men under fire. He learns about the varying personalities of the men who make up a nation's fighting forces: the braggart, the racist, the spiritual, the openly frightened, the perpetually angry. The army is everyman. As the action increases one senses the trauma of killing a human being: "I remembered looking down at him and feeling my own face torn apart . . ." (p. 182) One reads with compassion the unabashed sorrow displayed at the loss of a comrade—a fallen angel. The message is clear that Myers perceives war and killing not as a heroic event, but rather as a matter of survival.

In Myers' non-judgmental portrayal, the reader recognizes Perry's love for and understanding of the mother, who out of despair, turned to drink for solace. One feels the sense of protective responsibility for younger Kenny back in the WORLD, and for whom he hopes to make a better world. It is in this context that Myers, through Perry, poses the question of "WHY Vietnam?" and gives this response: "Having people care about you was probably the only thing that made any of this right." (p. 200) In this powerful war epic, the Perry who returns to Harlem is not the Perry who went to Vietnam, nor is the reader of *Fallen Angels* the same at the conclusion of the book. Each one is in Perry's words, "some other person than I was when I went to Nam . . ." (p. 316)

Walter Dean Myers has written a sobering book that will stand as classic among war stories, or any tale dealing with reflections on world social conditions.

Henrietta M. Smith
Delray Beach, Florida

In Nueva York by Nicholasa Mohr. Dial, 1977. 192 pages. (0-8037-4044-1) Arte Publico (University of Houston, Houston, TX, 77004), 1988. (pbk. 0-934770-78-6)

Eight interrelated short stories for young adults depict the way of life of several Puerto Rican neighbors on a block in New York's Lower East Side. Many of the same characters appear in several stories, with roles of greater or lesser importance in each. Although Spanish is used liberally throughout these stories, it is not set off in italics from the English text. The translation is instead embedded in the context, in a kind of print metaphor for the fusion of two cultures.

The stories in this collection are authentic and accurate not only in their depiction of the characters and their interactions with one another, but also in their evocation of the two Puerto Rican cultures that are present in the lives of all these characters. There is the culture "in Nueva York," in the run-down, dangerous, big-city neighborhood that is nonetheless full of caring, generous neighbors who find ways to enjoy and even celebrate life as they struggle to survive. But there is also the culture on the island of

Puerto Rico, a simple, trusting, safe way of life amid the nurturing love of family and the lushness of nature. The more remarkable stories in this collection, "Old Mary," "The English Lesson," and "Lali", convincingly depict the pulls of these two Puerto Rican cultures on the characters. The stories are complex, loving, and honest in their portrayal of the Puerto Rican spirit to survive and, most importantly, to exult in life.

Ana Nuncio
Needham, Massachusetts

Children's Multicultural Literature Resources

We direct your attention to the lists of works cited following each chapter in *The Multicolored Mirror*. These sources offer an abundance of resources for anyone wanting to continue to think about cultural authenticity in literature.

Articles and books by Multicolored Mirror conference leaders contribute provocative insights to the ongoing dialogue. Articles by writers and critics such as Walter Dean Myers, Doris Seale, Rudine Sims (Bishop) and Laurence Yep can be located in back issues of the *Bulletin* of the Council on Interracial Books for Children. Although the book examples in some articles may be from an earlier decade, the premise from which each author wrote offers much to consider and discuss. Look for their names on other published articles and books, as well. In particular, we urge you to locate *Shadow and Substance* by Rudine Sims (Bishop), a summary of her study of 150 books about African-Americans published between 1965 and 1980, to which we frequently turn for insight and information.

In addition to the works by conference speakers and other contributors to this book, we commend the published works of many colleagues whose leadership we value and from whom we continue to seek constructive resources. Anyone wanting to pursue this subject may wish to give new or renewed attention to the writings of Patricia F. Beilke and Frank J. Sciara, Violet J. Harris, Carla Hayden, Arlene Hirschfelder, Dianne Johnson, Donnarae MacCann, Donna E. Norton, Masha Rudman, Isabel Schon, Beverly Slapin, and Helen E. Williams.

Valuable resources not frequently cited include *The Slant of the Pen* (Preiswerk), *How Much Truth Do We Tell the Children?* (Bacon), and *Literature of American Minorities* in *The Lion and the Unicorn*, Volume 11, Number 1.

Specialized bookstores and library collections in and near college and university communities usually stock the materials suggested for courses in criticism and multicultural studies crossing the standard Eurocentric and Anglocentric boundaries. Browsing in such places will yield provocative reading about the ideas embraced within any consideration of cultural authenticity. For example, reading the anthology *Making Face, Making Soul/Haciendo Caras: Creative and Critical Perspectives of Women of Color* (Anzaldúa) leads one to *This Bridge Called My Back*, co-edited by the same writer.

Texts which survey children's and adolescent literature for undergraduate and graduate students offer increasingly substantial chapters about books reflecting a pluralistic society. Regardless of whether one agrees with each of the children's books recommended within the chapters, the listings of additional materials for adults which typically follow such chapters often yield citations of other related resources.

The following resource list is by no means comprehensive. Rather, it offers a starting place, from which a reader may branch out and find additional sources of relevant information. The list includes theoretical works as well as bibliographies of recommended children's and young adult books. You will read contradictory ideas. No one reader will agree with all of the views and opinions expressed. Ultimately, however, thoughtful consideration of resources such as these will enable one to examine one's own knowledge and biases, and, accordingly, re-evaluate how they influence one's selection and use of multicultural materials on behalf of children and adolescents.

Action Alliance for Children. *Children's Advocate*. (6 issues a year; $24.00/educational institutions and non-profit organizations; $18.00/individuals) Children's Advocate, Hunt House, 1201 Martin Luther King, Jr. Way, Oakland, CA 94612-1217.

Anzaldúa, Gloria, editor. *Making Face, Making Soul / Haciendo Caras: Creative and Critical Perspectives by Women of Color*. Aunt Lute Foundation Books, 1990. 402 pages. (pbk. 0-933216-73-4)

Bacon, Betty, editor. *How Much Truth Do We Tell the Children? The Politics of Children's Literature*. MEP Publications, 1988. 257 pages. (pbk. 0-930656-56-3)

Beilke, Patricia F. and Frank J. Sciara. *Selecting Materials for and about Hispanic and East Asian Children and Young People*. Library Professional Publications/Shoe String Press, 1986. 178 pages. (0-208-01993-6)

Council on Interracial Books for Children. *Bulletin*. (8 issues a year; $28.00/institutions; $20.00/individuals) CIBC, 1841 Broadway, New York, NY 10023.

Derman-Sparks, Louise and the A.B.C. Task Force. *Anti-Bias Curriculum: Tools for Empowering Young Children*. National Association for the Education of Young Children, 1989. 149 pages. (pbk. 0-935989-20-X)

Guidelines for Selecting Bias-free Textbooks and Storybooks. Council on Interracial Books for Children, 1980. 105 pages. (pbk. 0-930040-33-3)

Harris, Violet J. "Multicultural Curriculum: African American Children's Literature" in Research in Review column in *Young Children*, Vol. 46, No. 2, January 1991: 37-44. Published by the National Association for the Education of Young Children.

Hirschfelder, Arlene B. *American Indian Stereotypes in the World of Children: A Reader and Bibliography*. Scarecrow Press, 1982. 296 pages. (0-8108-1494-3)

Horning, Kathleen T. *Alternative Press Publishers of Children's Books: A Directory.* 4th edition. Friends of the CCBC, Inc. (Send a self-addressed, stamped envelope with inquiry c/o Publications, Friends of the CCBC, Inc., P.O. Box 5288, Madison, WI 53705), 1991. (pbk.)

Jenkins, Esther C. and Mary C. Austin. *Literature for Children about Asians and Asian Americans: Analysis and Annotated Bibliography, with Additional Readings for Adults.* Greenwood Press, 1987. 304 pages. (0-313-25970-4)

Johnson, Dianne. *Telling Tales: The Pedagogy and Promise of African American Literature for Youth.* Greenwood, 1990. 166 pages. (0-313-27206-9)

Kruse, Ginny Moore, and Kathleen T. Horning. *Multicultural Literature for Children and Young Adults: A Selected Listing of Books 1980-1990 by and about People of Color.* 3rd edition. Cooperative Children's Book Center, University of Wisconsin-Madison / Wisconsin Department of Public Instruction, 1991. 78 pages. (Available from Publication Sales, Wisconsin Department of Public Instruction, P.O. Box 7841, Madison, WI 53707-7841. Telephone 1-800-243-8782). pbk.

Kuipers, Barbara J. *American Indian Reference Books for Children and Young Adults.* Libraries Unlimited, 1991. 176 pages. (0-87287-745-0)

Literature of American Minorities in *The Lion and the Unicorn: A Critical Journal of Children's Literature.* Vol. 11, No. 1. Johns Hopkins University Press, 1987.

MacCann, Donnarae, and Gloria Woodard, editors. *The Black American in Books for Children: Readings in Racism.* Scarecrow Press, 1972. 223 pages. (0-8108-0526-X)

———. *Cultural Conformity* in *Books for Children: Further Readings in Racism.* Scarecrow Press, 1977. 205 pages. (0-8108-1064-6)

Multicultural Publishers Exchange. *Newsletter.* (6 issues a year; free to MPE members; $48.00/all others) Praxis Publications, P.O. Box 9869, Madison, WI 53715

Preiswerk, Roy, editor. *The Slant of the Pen: Racism in Children's Books.* Programme to Combat Racism, World Council of Churches, 1980. 154 pages. (pbk. 2-8254-0620-1)

Racism and Sexism in Children's Books. Writers and Readers, 1979. 147 pages. (pbk. 0-906495-18-0)

Rethinking Schools. (6 issues a year; $25.00/institutions; $10.00/individual; $5.00/student, unemployed) Rethinking Schools, 1001 E. Keefe Ave., Milwaukee, WI 53212

Rollock, Barbara. *Black Authors and Illustrators of Books for Children: A Biographical Dictionary.* Revised edition. Garland, 1992. 130 pages. (0-8240-7078-X)

Schon, Isabel. *A Bicultural Heritage: Themes for the Exploration of Mexican and Mexican-American Culture in Books for Children and Adolescents.* Scarecrow Press, 1978. 158 pages. (0-8108-1128-6)

———. *A Hispanic Heritage: A Guide to Juvenile Books about Hispanic People and Cultures.* Scarecrow Press, 1980. 168 pages. (0-8108-1290-8)

———. *A Hispanic Heritage, Series II: A Guide to Juvenile Books about Hispanic People and Cultures*. Scarecrow Press, 1985. 153 pages. (0-8108-1727-6)

———. *A Hispanic Heritage, Series III: A Guide to Juvenile Books about Hispanic People and Cultures*. Scarecrow Press, 1988. 150 pages. (0-8108-2133-8)

Sims, Rudine. *Shadow & Substance: Afro-American Experience in Contemporary Children's Fiction*. National Council of Teachers of English, 1982. 111 pages. (pbk. 0-8141-4376-8)

Slapin, Beverly, and Doris Seale. *Through Indian Eyes: The Native Experience in Books for Children*. Volume 3. New Society Publishers, 1991. 336 pages. (pbk. 0-86571-213-1; hardcover 0-86571-212-3)

Slapin, Beverly, and Doris Seale and Rosemary Gonzales. *How to Tell the Difference: A Checklist for Evaluating Native American Children's Books*. New Society Publishers, 1991. 32 pages. (pbk. 0-86571-214-X; hardcover 0-86571-215-8)

Verrall, Catherine, and Patricia McDowell, compilers. *Resource Reading List 1990: Annotated Bibliography of Resources by and about Native People*. Canadian Alliance in Solidarity with the Native Peoples (P.O. Box 574 Stn. P, Toronto, Ontario M5S 2T1, Canada), 1990. 150 pages. (pbk. 0-921425-03-1)

Williams, Helen E. *Books by African-American Authors and Illustrators for Children and Young Adults*. American Library Association, 1991. 270 pages. (0-8389-0570-6)

Appendix A

The Multicolored Mirror Institute
for Writers and Artists

A little over twenty years ago a group of concerned human beings addressed the question of the exclusion of people of color in children's literature. When confronted with this issue, the publishing industry offered the defense — perhaps objection is a better word — that they would gladly publish people of color *if only* they could find people who were publishable.

In response, the Council on Interracial Books for Children conducted a contest. The monetary prize for those annual contests were extremely modest: five hundred dollars. But the prize to the writers who responded was enormous. Not only were we being noticed, we were even being solicited. The winners of those annual contests, people like Sharon Bell Mathis, Kristin Hunter, Virginia Driving Hawk Sneve, and me, were introduced to publishing and publishing was introduced to a new multicultural world.

The problem of people of color being represented in children's literature is still with us. So, too, are the people who are interested in solving the problem. The rationale now, as it was 20 years ago, is not to simply have more people published; it is an effort to end the exclusion of children from the full richness of the human experience.

One of the answers, or at least the answer being offered by the Cooperative Children's Book Center, was the Multicolored Mirror Institute. Quite simply, the Institute was a seminar in which selected African-American, Asian, Native American, and Latino writers and artists were brought together with teams of multicultural writers who have already made professional inroads. The Institute held this April was fantastic, as were the new artists and writers we encountered. It was our answer to *if only* they could find people who were publishable. They are.

Walter Dean Myers, chair
Multicolored Mirror Institute for Writers and Artists

Background Information

The idea for the Institute developed over a period of three years, following informal conversations Ginny Moore Kruse and Kathleen T. Horning, both of the Cooperative Children's Book Center, University of Wisconsin - Madison, had with children's authors Walter Dean Myers and Mavis Jukes, and artists Tom Feelings and Robert Hudson following a children's literature conference, "In the Wake of Home," which all of the above-mentioned attended in Madison, Wisconsin. All of us felt compelled to do something about the appallingly low numbers of juvenile trade books published each year which are written and/or illustrated by people of color (less than two percent of the titles published each year, although early figures in the 1990 census project about 25 percent of the U.S. population identify themselves as African-American, American Indian, Asian-American, or Hispanic/Latino).

As our conversations with each other continued and expanded to include others, we finally decided to hold an Institute for unpublished writers and artists, which would give them an opportunity to come together and learn from experienced children's book writers, illustrators and editors. We planned to hold a day-long Institute following our biennial two-day children's literature conference on multicultural literature.

In the spring of 1990, we applied for and received a grant from the University of Wisconsin - Extension/Curriculum and Program Development Initiative. This grant provided the necessary funds for the Institute, which included paying all expenses for 20 fellowship recipients and six mentors. An advisory committee made up of local artists and writers of color worked with us as we prepared a press release, an application form, and began to plan the Institute content and structure. In addition to providing their insights as writers and artists, members of the advisory committee also critiqued our work for unconscious cultural biases and shared information about how to tap into networks already in place within communities of color.

We prepared a press release announcing the availability of fellowships, which was mailed out to newspapers and periodicals operated by people of color, Black colleges, Indian tribal offices and community colleges, and writers and artists groups. We received roughly 200 queries from individuals asking for an application form and 88 formal applications from writers and artists all over the U.S. The applicants were asked to submit samples of their writing and/or artwork. Each submission was judged and rated by writer Walter Dean Myers, writer/publisher Wade Hudson, and artist/writer/publisher Cheryl Willis Hudson. The top twenty applicants were awarded fellowships.

The fellowship recipients traveled to Madison, Wisconsin, on April 4, 1991, and attended the children's literature conference, "The Multicolored Mirror," on April 5-6, along with 250 children's librarians, teachers, and other adults interested in children's literature. On April 7, they attended a day-long Institute, led by Walter Dean Myers, Wade and Cheryl Hudson, Tom Feelings, editor Phoebe Yeh, and writer Gary Soto. In an informal, small-group setting, they had an opportunity to learn from each other and ask questions about writing and illustrating books for children.

All in all, we hope that our efforts will have some impact on the children's book publishing world and that, in the years to come, we will see a broader, more realistic representation of our diverse society in books for children and teenagers.

Kathleen T. Horning, Institute coordinator
Cooperative Children's Book Center

Jane Pearlmutter, Institute program administrator
UW School of Library and Information Studies/Continuing Education Services

INSTITUTE MENTORS

Walter Dean Myers, chair
Tom Feelings
Cheryl Hudson
Wade Hudson
Gary Soto
Phoebe Yeh

FELLOWSHIP AWARDS JURY

Cheryl Hudson
Wade Hudson
Walter Dean Myers

LOCAL ADVISORY COMMITTEE

Cathy Caldwell, writer
Barbara Golden, writer
Karen Martin, writer
Noemi Mendoza, writer
Charles Taylor, publisher
Freida High Tesfagiorgis, artist

INSTITUTE PARTICIPANTS

AFRICAN

Writer
Innocent Banda
Madison, WI

AFRICAN-AMERICAN

Writers
Akindele Akinde
Washington, DC

Jonetta Rose Barras
Washington, DC

Jacqueline Francis
Madison, WI

Barbara Golden *
Madison, WI

Esther Hall Mumford
Seattle, WA

Carletta Wilson
Seattle, WA

Patricia Young
Brooklyn, NY

Artists
Ovid P. Adams
Honolulu, HI

Michael Bryant
Newark, NJ

Ira Harmon
Chicago, IL

ASIAN-AMERICAN

Writer
June Kuzuko Inuzuka
Denver, CO

Writer/Artist
Nancy Lee
Seattle, WA

AMERICAN INDIAN

Writers
Cathy Caldwell *
Stevens Point, WI

David DePoe
Cloquet, MN

Genevieve Gollnick
Oneida, WI

Karen Martin *
Madison, WI

AMERICAN INDIAN

Artists
Patricia DePoe
Cloquet, MN

Victoria Doud
Lac du Flambeau, WI

Ouapiti Robintree
Eugene, OR

LATINO/A

Writers
Jack Agueros
New York, NY

Irene B. Hernandez
Duncanville, TX

H. Emilia Paredes
Oakland, CA

* Member of local Advisory Committee

The Multicolored Mirror
Institute for Writers and Artists

April 7, 1991

Schedule

9:00 - 10:00 a.m.
Overview of the current juvenile publishing industry — Walter Dean Myers

10:00 - 10:15
Break

10:15 - 11:00
Forum — Cheryl and Wade Hudson, Walter Dean Myers, Gary Soto, Phoebe Yeh

An opportunity for participants to respond to what they've heard and seen over the past few days and to ask questions of the Institute leaders in general.

11:00 - 12:00 p.m.
Small Groups:
1. Writing — Gary Soto 2. Writing — Walter Dean Myers 3. Writing — Wade Hudson 4. Illustrating — Tom Feelings 5. Illustrating — Cheryl Hudson 6. Writing and Illustrating — Phoebe Yeh

12:00 - 1:15
Lunch and Browsing Time

1:15 - 2:00
Editors' panel — Cheryl Hudson, Wade Hudson, Phoebe Yeh
What do publishers look for? Who is responsible for accuracy — the editor or author/illustrator? How to prepare and submit a manuscript or portfolio

2:15 - 3:00
Small Groups (Break out as above)

3:00 - 4:00
Informal Networking (an opportunity for participants and leaders to mingle freely)

4:00 - 4:15
Closing

Appendix B

The Multicolored Mirror Planning Committee

April 5-6, 1991
University of Wisconsin - Madison

Conference Planning Committee

Dianne Hopkins
School of Library and Information Studies
University of Wisconsin - Madison

Kathleen T. Horning
Cooperative Children's Book Center
University of Wisconsin - Madison

John M. Kean
School of Education
University of Wisconsin - Madison

Ginny Moore Kruse
Cooperative Children's Book Center
University of Wisconsin - Madison

Merri V. Lindgren
Cooperative Children's Book Center
University of Wisconsin - Madison

Jane Pearlmutter
School of Library and Information Studies Continuing Education Services
University of Wisconsin - Madison

Holly G. Willett
School of Library and Information Studies
University of Wisconsin - Madison

Facilitators of Small Group Book Discussions

Joan Airoldi
Northern Waters Library Service
Ashland, Wisconsin

Cathy Caldwell
Stevens Point, Wisconsin

Vernette Crum
Milwaukee Public Schools
Milwaukee, Wisconsin

Dorothy Davids
Full Circle/Multicultural Education
Gresham, Wisconsin

Barbara Golden
Madison, Wisconsin

Ruth Gudinas
Full Circle/Multicultural Education
Gresham, Wisconsin

Carla Hayden
Chicago Public Library
Chicago, Illinois

Josephine Hill
Milwaukee Public Schools
Milwaukee, Wisconsin

Maureen Holmes
Waukesha Public Library
Waukesha, Wisconsin

Renée Hoxie
Madison Metropolitan School District
Madison, Wisconsin

Karen Martin
Madison, Wisconsin

Henrietta Smith
University of South Florida-Tampa
Delray Beach, Florida

Holly Willett
University of Wisconsin - Madison
Madison, Wisconsin

Ann Wilson
Wingra School
Madison, Wisconsin